The Diet is DEAD

Why traditional diets fail and how you can succeed.

By Daniel Reynen and the Women and Men of WeBeFit.com.

Cover design by: The WeBeFit.com Research Team

FIRST EDITION

Inquiries should be addressed to:

WeBeFit Personal Training
1277 1st Street, Suite 1
Key West, Florida 33040

www.TheDietisDead.com
www.DietisDead.com
www.WeBeFit.com

LIBRARY OF CONGRESS
CATALOGING IN PUBLICATION DATA

Eden Entertainment Limited, Inc.
The Diet is Dead
First Edition

Printed in the United States of America

ISBN 978-0-9672819-8-8

The Diet is Dead

Written by
Daniel Reynen
and the Women and Men
of WeBeFit.com.

1/2011

Contents

Introduction
How it Works

"I know what I'm supposed to eat, my body only craves what it needs." That's what a client told me when I started questioning her about her diet.

This was a woman (I'll call her Tina) more than 100 pounds overweight, telling me what she was eating wasn't the problem. Tina was convinced her diet was healthy. She believed her body "instinctively" knew the right things to eat and all she had to do was listen.

At 100 pounds overweight, apparently some signals were getting crossed.

The mistaken belief that our bodies somehow "know" what they need is something I regularly hear from my personal training clients. The reality is our bodies have been finely tuned to survive without a refrigerator, a convenience store down the street or 24-hour fast food joints.

Here's why those things are such a problem. If you're relying on instinct, your body's telling you to avoid exercise (because muscle burns more calories than fat), eat as much as possible and put on weight because you never know when you'll get your next meal.

It appears the majority of Americans are following those instincts.

If this were a diet book, we would tell you that everything you know is wrong. We'd say the best way to lose weight is to follow our program. Then we'd give you some simple food plans — branded with our logo, and available at your local grocery store — with just enough calories to keep you conscious, but not much else. If fashion designers took this same no-frills approach, we'd all be wearing nothing more than white housecoats and paper shoes.

The reason we say the Diet is Dead is because changes like that work, for a little while, but they rarely produce lasting results. You lose the weight, your metabolism drops and then when you resume your regular eating habits you pack on even more pounds. Instead of a diet, ours is a system that teaches you how to figure out what YOUR body needs, not what we want you to eat, or want you to buy.

The downside is that it will require more effort from you. When we were putting this book together, we were told repeatedly that it was too technical. We were told we should dumb things down and tell the reader exactly what to do, instead of explaining how each person should calculate what's best for them as individuals. We should, essentially, issue our readers their very own WeBeFit white housecoats and paper shoes. No thinking allowed!

We didn't do that. The nutritional needs of a vegan who swims three hours a week and works a desk job is quite different from a meat lover who works construction and runs marathons. If you want generic advice, there are plenty of books that already offer that. We're going to share the details and the science to back it up. Here's what's in this book.

We start with a little lesson in personality. We'll tell you why big dramatic changes often fail. Then we'll tell you how to make small changes that last.

The next section is figuring out just what kind of shape you're in: How big your waist should be, how fast or slow your metabolism is working and how much fat you might be carrying around.

After that we help you calculate what your body needs: How many calories you should eat, how much protein is appropriate and facts about fiber, carbs and fat.

Then there's a lesson on how to read a nutrition label fast. When you go shopping you'll quickly be able to figure out which foods are okay and which ones you should swap out with healthier alternatives.

Once you know what to look for, we'll help you keep track of it all. There are several options including paper logs, computer software, phone programs and even meal plans for when you're short on time.

That's followed by chapters on how to get through a grocery store, organize your refrigerator and clean out your kitchen. These are practical steps you can take to save time, money and surround yourself with healthier options.

The final sections of the book are dedicated to helping you cope with some of life's challenges. What you can do when you're on a plane, over the holidays and how to handle a party. Advice you can put to use immediately when temptation appears like a devil on your shoulder.

Our goal is to teach you how to make educated decisions about what you eat and set goals that are attainable, sustainable and safe. We will only share with you clinically proven and medically researched facts to help you make healthier decisions.

Take things one-step at a time and keep going over each chapter until you're comfortable with the information. It's not a quick fix; it's about lasting change.

Disclaimer

The advice offered in this book is not intended to be a substitute for the advice and counsel of a personal physician, licensed nutritionist or health care provider.

How to Read this Book

This book contains a lot of information. If you try and read it all at once, it can be overwhelming. To help you out, we've broken it down into small chunks.

Start by reading no more than one chapter a day. When there's a lot to learn, we'll give you the most important points right at the beginning of a chapter. Then we'll go into more detail to make sure you're comfortable with the information.

At the end of each chapter is a summary of things we really want you to remember and an assignment. We give you specific actions to take. By putting the information you learn to work, you're more likely to remember and use it to make your life healthier.

 When you see the STOP sign, do the assignment before moving on.

 The CALCULATOR appears when you need to figure something out.

If you don't understand something, take the time to go back and read it again. If it still doesn't make sense, visit our website at www.DietisDead.com where we'll post the most frequently asked questions with more detailed explanations.

Our goal with this book is to help you understand how to make healthier food choices. This is not an exercise book. We won't be giving you routines or describing various workout programs. While we understand exercise is a critical component of overall health, there's simply not enough room for us to include that information here. If you're looking for workout routines and advice, please visit our website www.WeBeFit.com.

When you're ready, take your time, slowly reading each chapter, doing the assignments and change the way you approach food forever.

Taking Action

There are three essential parts of a successful diet and exercise program:

Knowledge, Motivation and Action.

You have to learn about healthy eating and proper exercise, get excited about making a change and take steps to put a plan in motion. For most people getting started isn't the problem, it's sticking with it.

We are essentially creatures of habit. The foods we enjoy eating, the clothes we like wearing, even the feelings we have every day are heavily influenced by what we've learned as we grew up. If you were raised in an environment where healthy food was the norm and exercise was encouraged, there's a good chance you eat healthy food and exercise regularly.

By the same token, if a family outing consisted of hitting the drive thru because the walk from the parking lot was too much effort, chances are those ideas are still shaping your decisions today. Changing those bad habits can be extremely difficult and personality can hamper your ability to change. But this is where we begin.

Psychologists can describe most character traits using five dimensions:

Agreeableness
Conscientiousness
Extroversion
Neuroticism
Openness

Personality tests are used to measure and see if people are "high" or "low" on each dimension. For example, someone who scores high on agreeableness is considered friendly and warm while a low agreeableness score indicates someone who is shy or suspicious.

In 2003 Psychologist Sanjay Srivastava Ph.D. and his colleagues assessed the "Big Five" personality traits of more than 130,000 participants.[1] What they discovered is that openness, the personality trait linked to a person's willingness to make change, increases modestly in people up to the age of 30. After that it begins a slow decline. Things outside our normal range of experience become increasingly less attractive.[2]

What that means is we are wired to slowly slip into a rut after age 30 and we're content to stay there. In fact, the more we insist we can change in spite of past failures, the more likely it is we'll ultimately fail again. It's called the "false hope syndrome." You've probably experienced it in your life. Here's how it works.

It's New Years day and you resolve that this is the year you're going to start exercising and eat right. That's good. The problem is underestimating the difficulty involved and overestimating the benefits. Here is an example of what you might say, and then deep down what you're thinking.

You say, *"I resolve to go on a diet and lose 20 pounds."*

You think, *"I'm going on a diet to lose 20 pounds **and then I'll get a better job.**"*

---

1. Sanjay Srivastava, Ph.D., and Oliver P. John, Ph.D., University of California, Berkeley; Samuel D. Gosling, Ph.D., University of Texas, Austin; Jeff Potter, B.A., Cambridge, MA. *Development of Personality in Early and Middle Adulthood: Set Like Plaster or Persistent Change?* Journal of Personality and Social Psychology, Vol. 84, No. 5. May 2003.

2. For more detailed information on personality traits, we suggest reading John, O. P., Naumann, L. P., & Soto, C. J. *Handbook of Personality: Theory and Research* starting at chapter 4, Paradigm Shift to the Integrative Big-Five Trait Taxonomy: History, Measurement, and Conceptual Issues. Edited by: O. P. John, R. W. Robins, & L. A. Pervin (pp. 114-158). Guilford Press: New York, NY. 2008.

Steps to Change

What does it take to make a successful change in your life? Psychologists have identified two primary ways to make successful long-term changes.

The first way is through a traumatic event.

The death of a loved one, a life threatening illness, the beginning or end of a relationship, a change in jobs, a natural catastrophe or move are all things that shake people out of their comfort zone. When something traumatic happens, you're forced to do things differently. People who survive the trauma are often able to redefine themselves and make significant changes. But before you start plotting the "lose weight through disaster" diet, there's another way.

The second way is through small steps.

All learning is a pattern of steps. After all, Arnold Schwarzenegger didn't come out of the womb muscle-bound, for which his mother must be extremely grateful. Mozart didn't start writing symphonies when he was a kid... wait, bad example.

Good habits are built, much like buildings, one brick at a time. They do not magically appear. For most people, there are just too many habits to break all at once to make a big resolution stick. But if you break it down into something manageable, decide to make just one change at a time, your chances for success rise dramatically. Take small bites, as your mother may have said the first time you had spaghetti noodles hanging from your mouth. Here's how.

STEP ONE – Focus on one thing.

Start by picking a single healthy pledge for yourself. Get a card and write down one of the things from the list you made at the end of the Taking Action chapter. Go ahead and get that card now. This book will wait.

Front Side of Card

Back Side of Card

> I will eat three servings
> of vegetables a day.
>   1/1/2011

> To get more naturally
> occuring vitamins and
> minerals.

Now you're going to concentrate on ONE thing and work at it until you're comfortable and it's become as much a routine as eating or sleeping.

For example: Instead of trying to eat only healthy food from now on, just try to change one food-related thing. Maybe you'll resolve to eat at least three servings of vegetables a day for a month. That's it. You don't have to stop eating everything you're used to. You can still be on a first name basis with the pizza delivery guy (for now). And it's okay to check in with the family that runs that great little Mexican place down the street, just so they don't file a missing persons report.

On the front side of the card you would write "I will eat three servings of vegetables a day." On the bottom, put the date to document when you started. Then put the card in your purse or wallet and carry it with you.

STEP TWO – Follow through daily.

Make sure you remember your pledge. On the back side of the card, you might write "To get more naturally occurring vitamins and minerals" or "To experience tastes I haven't tried before." Avoid statements that are negative. It's easier to work FOR something than AGAINST something.

Every day when you get up, read your card.

Then decide approximately when and where you are going to take action on it. If you resolved to eat more vegetables, you have to plan on when and where you'll get those vegetables in. You might put new things in a breakfast omelet; carry a bag of vegetable treats to lunch or experiment with a new vegetable dish for dinner.

Here's why it works. Carrying around that reminder every day, you'll be reading what you're supposed to do and why you're taking action. You've identified what needs to change. After 30 days, you've turned that one small step into a habit.

Sometimes carrying a card isn't enough. If you're someone who needs more constant attention, there's a very simple way to do it.

Get a tattoo.

Sorry, that's for the really tough cases. Before going extreme, pick up a rubber band or wrist-band. You probably already have one lying around the house. You're going to wear it, but the WAY you wear it is what will make the difference. Think of it as a bold life-changing fashion statement.

Instead of just putting it on as a mere reminder, you're going to use it strategically.

Start by saying your healthy choice out loud and then slip the wristband on your arm. Now you're committed. Whatever arm you put it on is where that wristband will stay until thirty days have passed OR you slip up.

One note of caution: Make sure it isn't too tight. Although cutting off your circulation and turning your hand blue would show a certain amount of devotion, picking up broccoli spears with a numb hand can be a problem.

If you break your promise, you have to move the wristband onto the opposite arm and start all over. Mark the new date on the calendar, make the pledge and start again.

This helps you succeed three different ways.

1. The wristband on your arm keeps reminding you of your goal.
2. You are less likely to succumb to temptation because that just means you'll have to move the wristband on the other side and start over.
3. After 30 days of doing something it tends to become a habit.

If the wristband doesn't work, then go for the tattoo. A tattoo that says "Eat three servings of vegetables a day" would be a real conversation starter around the gym.

STEP THREE – Give yourself another goal.

Once you've been successful with one choice, spend a couple days with the wristband off and decide what your next healthy choice should be. Set the date, make the pledge, fill out another card, slip the wristband on and build another good habit.

Over time, all those small changes add up. Here are three examples of healthy promises you can

Have problems getting out of bed in the morning? Don't get in bed at midnight if you want to wake up refreshed at 5:00 in the morning. Resolve to get in bed at least eight hours before you're supposed to get up. If that means skipping a little late night television or Internet surfing, then do it. If you live somewhere noisy, get earplugs and an alarm that shakes the bed.

HEALTHY PLEDGE: I will go to bed eight hours before I must get up.
REASON WHY: To wake up refreshed and alert.

Are you rushing out the door, skipping breakfast and eating junk food? Make a plan to get up 15 minutes earlier so you can have a proper breakfast. Buy some fat free milk and cereal with fiber. Have a little oatmeal. Scramble some egg whites. Have healthy choices available in your kitchen and give yourself some time when you wake up.

HEALTHY PLEDGE: I will eat breakfast every morning.
REASON WHY: To give myself energy to face the day.

Do you fight traffic and worry about parking when you go to work? On your day off, see how long it'll take if you walk, ride a bike or take the bus to your job. Walking and riding a bike can give you some exercise, taking the bus may save you money and give you time to relax while you're being driven around.

HEALTHY PLEDGE: Twice a week I will bike, bus or walk to work.
REASON WHY: Start the day with fresh air, relaxation and exercise.

STOP

TAKE ACTION:
Choose one of the goals you wrote down from the previous chapter. Carry it with you, read and act on it every day.

Summary
Steps to Change

Focus on One Thing

Get a card and write down one small (but specific) change you are going to make.

Follow Through

On the back side of the card write down a reason why you're making the change. Carry that card with you every day to constantly remind you of the change you're making and why you're doing it.

Remind yourself by putting a rubber wristband on one arm and keep it there for 30 days. If you slip up, move the wristband to the other arm and start over.

Give Yourself Another Goal

If you successfully achieve your goal for at least 30 days, plan the next one. Spend a day or two deciding what it should be and then write it down. Go back to the beginning and do it all over again.

Write It Down

Over the next several chapters you're going to figure a few things out. We're going to tell you how to measure, poke and prod your body to get an idea of the shape you're in.

Once you have all the numbers, we'll show you where they should be. The best way to make progress is by knowing where you are and where you need to be.

If you have access to a computer and printer, you can get most of this information online. We'll do the calculations for you and print out a sheet with all your information.

Go to www.DietisDead.com and click on the "All About YOU" link.

You can also use the formulas in the following chapter and figure the numbers out for yourself. The page labeled "All About Me Log" is where you're going to record all your information. Don't panic when you see the page! We're going to tell you, step-by-step how to fill out every part of it.

If this is a library book, a loaner from a friend or the sheet is already filled in, you can visit our website www.DietisDead.com and download blank sheets.

All About Me Log

Start Date _____

Waist-to-Hip Ratio	Now	60 Days	180 Days
Waist Measurement	___	___	___
Hip Measurement	___	___	___
Ratio	___	___	___

Women ideally want to have a waist-to-hip ratio below .80
Men should be below .95

Body Mass Index (BMI)	Now	60 Days	180 Days
	___	___	___

Body Mass Index (BMI) should equal about 22, but anything under 26 is healthy. Below 20 is considered underweight.

Body Fat Percentage	Now	60 Days	180 Days
	___	___	___

Women should be between 13 and 24%. 25-31% is accept-able. 32% and higher is obese. Below 13% may be underweight. Men should be between 5 and 17%. 18-25% is acceptable. 26% and higher is obese. Below 5% may be underweight.

Resting Metabolic Rate	Now	+/- 10 lbs	+/- 10 lbs.
	___	___	___

You should re-test after 10-15 pounds of weight change or every 9-12 months.

How many calories do you burn from exercise daily?			
	Now	60 Days	180 Days
	___	___	___

How much should you eat?	Now	60 Days	180 Days
How many CALORIES daily?	___	___	___
How much FAT daily?	___	___	___
How much SUGAR Daily?	___	___	___
How much PROTEIN daily?	___	___	___
How much FIBER daily?	___	___	___
How much SALT daily?	___	___	___

All About Me

Okay, here's the (potentially) bad news section of this journey. Human nature is opposed to getting bad news. We don't like hearing it, we don't like admitting it and we don't like when it's about us. Get ready for your splash of reality.

Over the past 40 years, Americans have been growing progressively larger. Deaths due to complications from obesity are continuing to rise. Unfortunately, everybody seems to think it's someone else who's gaining the weight.

The results of an obesity study[3] that polled 11,000 people was released in August of 2006. More than 75% of the obese respondents claimed to have healthy eating habits. 40% of those same people also said they engaged in "vigorous" exercise at least three times a week.

What the study indicates is that many people are in denial about their activities, perhaps thinking "vigorous" means "taking four stairs two at a time," and "healthy eating habits" means "eating only half the fries that came with the Triple Humongoburger and Soda."

Without a doctor's advice, it's easy to keep telling ourselves it's everyone else...we don't have a problem. We're not one of the statistics. Nobody is secretly filming us at the mall for stock obesity footage. Oh yeah, and we're all great drivers too.

Taking health seriously means starting with honesty. We must take responsibility for our actions as well as our inactions. A major component of the False Hope Syndrome, mentioned in the Taking Action chapter is an

---

3. Telephone Survey of 11,000 people conducted by: Thomson Medstat, January – March 2006.

unwillingness to be accountable for the behaviors that need changing, and the consequences of those behaviors.

It's time to hear the truth. Let's look at three bits of information that will help you begin to determine honestly what kind of shape you're in. It will only take a minute, the first two are free, and you do not need to insert yourself into any special equipment. Skip the math. You can do this online at www.DietisDead.com. Click on the "All About YOU" link.

1 – Waist-to-Hip Ratio

Researchers came up with this test after they discovered that just having a little extra weight isn't always a problem. It's how that weight is distributed on your body that can make a big difference. An extra five pounds isn't a big deal; an extra five pounds on your eyelids is.

Younger women tend to be more bottom heavy. That means they gain weight in their hips, thighs and bottoms. Researchers call this a "pear" shape. As women age and go through menopause, the weight starts to shift and re-distribute around the middle, just like men. Not coincidentally, it's around menopause that female death rate for heart disease catches up with men.

Men tend to have their weight mostly concentrated around the midsection, giving them an "apple" shape. Having an apple shape puts you at higher risk for heart disease than the pear shape, so researchers use the waist-to-hip ratio measurements to determine your body's shape and risk.

The only thing you'll need to find out your waist-to-hip ratio is a tape measure.

HOW TO MEASURE – Waist

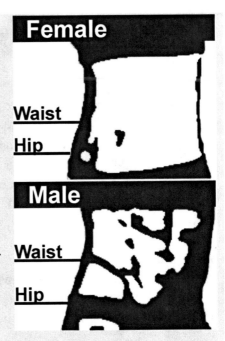

Men start and finish at the naval. Women should measure midway between the bottom of the ribs and the top of the hip bone. Take the measurement in inches or centimeters while standing relaxed, no sucking the belly in!

HOW TO MEASURE – Hips

Men need to measure at the tip of the hip bone. Women should start measuring at the widest point between the hips and buttocks.

_____ ÷ _____ = _____

Waist Measure ÷ Hip Measure = Waist/Hip Ratio

Here's an example: If your waist measures 26 inches around and your hips are 33 inches, you would divide 26 by 33. The answer is .78.

Women should be below .80
Men should be below .95

If your number is higher than that, you are at a much higher risk of weight-related health problems including diabetes, hypertension and heart problems. If you find yourself near or above those danger numbers, you need to take steps today to start losing the fat.

Without even considering the ratio, if you're a man and your waistline is 40 inches or more, your risk of heart related problems is considered high. For women the cutoff number is 35 inches. Get out a tape measure; find out what your number is. If you're near or above the danger zone, then it's time to take action and fix it. Unlike other health related measurements, the lowest healthy number is not currently known for waist-to-hip ratio. If you're concerned about being underweight, use the next section to find out.

2 – Body Mass Index (BMI)

Body Mass Index or BMI is a measure of general fitness and health.[4] Getting yourself to the right number can add ONE YEAR to your life. If you're just 10 pounds overweight, you may be cutting your life short by up to 12 months. Only 10 extra pounds may be more hazardous to your cardiovascular health than either diabetes or living with a smoker.

You could add an entire year! What would you do with the time? Finish the life-sized Lego castle in the backyard? Take out the garbage 104 more times? Here's how to figure out your BMI. Remember we'll calcualte it for you at www.DietisDead.com under the "All About YOU" link.

British researchers discovered the lowest combined rate of heart disease, diabetes, strokes, and even death occurred in people whose BMI was between 20 and 23.9. Once your BMI gets higher than that, disease and death rates start rising about 10 percent per index point - or about every six to eight pounds for most people (depending on height).

Your BMI is determined by dividing your weight (in kilograms) by the square of your height (in meters). But we've got an easier way that doesn't require any math.

On the next page is a height/weight table so you can quickly look up what your ideal weight should be. Remember the table shows a RANGE. If you are outside the range you need to take steps to get back in.

---

4. Dympna Gallagher, Steven B Heymsfield, Moonseong Heo, Susan A Jebb, Peter R Murgatroyd and Yoichi Sakamoto. *Healthy percentage body fat ranges: an approach for developing guidelines based on body mass index.* From the Obesity Research Center, St Luke's–Roosevelt Hospital, Columbia University College of Physicians and Surgeons, New York, NY; MRC Human Nutrition Research, Cambridge, United Kingdom; and Kashiwa Hospital, Jikei University, Chiba, Japan. American Journal of Clinical Nutrition: Vol. 72, No. 3, 694-701, September 2000.

Height in Feet & Inches	Men (Pounds)	Women (Pounds)
4' 8"	90-112	83-106
4' 9"	93-116	86-110
4' 10"	96-120	89-114
4' 11"	100-124	93-118
5'	103-128	96-122
5' 1"	106-132	99-126
5' 2"	110-137	102-130
5' 3"	113-141	106-134
5' 4"	117-146	109-139
5' 5"	121-150	112-143
5' 6"	125-155	116-147
5' 7"	128-160	119-152
5' 8"	132-164	123-157
5' 9"	136-169	127-161
5' 10"	140-174	130-166
5' 11"	144-179	134-171
6'	148-184	138-175
6' 1"	152-189	142-180
6' 2"	157-195	146-185
6' 3"	161-200	150-190
6' 4"	165-205	154-196

UNDER THE RANGE - Thin may be in, but being too thin can actually be unhealthy. Women primarily fall in this category but it's not unheard of in men. Extreme cases may lead to anorexia, muscle wasting, bone degeneration and even death. If you are under the range, it's time to take steps and put on some healthy weight.

WITHIN THE RANGE - Congratulations. You are in a very select group. Your weight is considered ideal. You should concentrate on healthy eating and daily exercise to keep yourself in that range.

ABOVE THE RANGE – It's time to start losing weight. Read on and over the next few chapters, we'll give you diet tips to get the best long-term results.

Calculate your BMI manually and get an exact number by following the steps below.

1. Convert your body weight to kilograms.

_____ ÷ **2.2 =** _____
body weight (in pounds) ÷ by 2.2 = weight in kilograms
Take your body weight (in pounds) and divide it by 2.2. The answer is your weight in kilograms.

2. Convert your height to meters

_____ ÷ **39.37 =** _____
height (inches) ÷ by 39.37 = height in meters
Measure your height (in inches) and divide it by 39.37 to get your height in meters.

3. Calculate BMI

_____ ÷ (_____ x _____) = _____
weight in kilograms ÷ by (height in meters x height in meters) = BMI
Multiply your height in meters by your height in meters. Yes it's the same number, that's not a typo. The answer is your multiplied height. Now divide your weight in kilograms by your multiplied height. The final answer is your Body Mass Index.

The results are:
　　　You are Underweight if your BMI is lower than 18.5
　　　Normal weight if your BMI is 18.5 to 24.9
　　　Overweight if your BMI is 25 to 29.9
　　　Obese if your BMI is 30 or greater

The most common question we get about BMI is this: *"But, I'm a body-builder, does this really apply to me?"* Yes. You can get away with a higher BMI, but even for bodybuilders, a BMI over 30 isn't healthy.

How about weighing myself?

The scale is generally NOT a good indicator of health. For example, let's say two women both weigh 155 pounds.

"Beth" may have 60 pounds of body fat and 95 pounds of lean body mass, while "Ann" may have 35 pounds of body fat and 120 pounds of lean body mass. They both weigh the same but "Ann" is in much better shape because she has more lean body mass and less body fat.

3 – Body Fat Percentage

Your body is made up of essential and stored fats.

Essential fats are needed for proper body functioning. They help you process vitamins A, D, E, and K, because these vitamins are fat-soluble. (Fat-soluble means the body must use fat to properly absorb them.)

Stored fats help provide warmth and protection for your body. Your muscles also use stored fats for energy. Problems begin when you have excess body fat. To understand how much fat is too much, check out the following table.

	Women	Men
Essential Fat	10-12%	2-4%
Athletes	13-20%	5-13%
Fitness	21-24%	14-17%
Acceptable	25-31%	18-25%
Obese	32% & Higher	25% & Higher

The numbers break down like this: If you go below the levels of Essential Fats, you risk conditions like osteoporosis, a dangerous thinning of bone. Women can also have their menstrual cycles interrupted and even grow a layer of body hair as a means for the body to warm itself in the absence of healthy body fat.

Ideally you should be in the Athlete or Fitness range. If you're in this range, you significantly reduce your chances of experiencing serious medical conditions, like heart attack, stroke and some cancers.

If you're in the Acceptable range, you should consider it a polite tap on the shoulder to look closer at your health, especially if you're at the higher end of the Acceptable range. You aren't automatically at risk, but you are more likely to experience health problems than people in the Athlete or Fitness range.

Finally, consider the Overweight or Obese range a warning sign. You should immediately talk to your doctor or health care professional about improving your diet and fitness. Simply moving from the Obese to Acceptable category can potentially add years to your life.

How to test body fat.

This test does involve some not-so-common apparatus, but it is not a medieval torture device. The well-known ones anyway. There are two common ways of testing body fat. The first is **skin-fold measurement**, where a person uses calipers to measure specific spots on your body. These measurements are compared to a chart that show the estimated body fat percentage. Unfortunately this method is only as accurate and consistent as the person administering the test.

The second common method is **bioelectric impedance (BIA)**. BIA works by sending an electrical charge through the body. The resistance to the charge is measured and an estimate of your body fat is calculated.

Both types of body fat tests are generally available from local gyms, health clubs and personal trainers.

Because both common methods have an error range as low as 2%, to as high as 8%, it is best to be tested at least twice, under the same conditions each time.

Once you have your initial number, you should test yourself monthly, to make sure your exercise program has you losing fat, not muscle. If you're happy with your current body fat percentage, and fat/muscle ratio, a test every three or four months will tell you if you're maintaining it.

TAKE ACTION:
Write down all your information in the log on page 31. For blank forms and help calculating visit www.DietisDead.com.

How Much Should I Eat?

Now that you've determined your waist-to-hip ratio, body mass index and body fat percentage, you have a better idea of what kind of shape your body's in.

The next step is figuring out how much you should be eating. If this were a typical diet book, we would post a weeks worth of menus and restrict your calories to 1,200 a day. That's the number you can safely recommend people eat without requiring a doctor's oversight.

We would also throw in some kind of hook. For example we might say you have to eliminate most of your carbs, just eat raw vegetables, or load up on large amounts of protein. The hooks are there to get your attention and provide easy rules to follow.

The problem with these restrictive diets is you eat things that aren't necessarily a part of your daily life. So they work, for awhile, but eventually real life interferes and you're back to eating familiar foods at the same elevated levels as before.

Most people remember the hook (I say Atkins, you say Low Carb!) but few realize that no matter what diet you choose, it's all about reducing the calories. It's simple. To lose weight, eat less than your body burns.

The question is, how much less should you eat? If you're one of those who want to put on weight you need to eat more, but how much more?

It's time to learn a magic number: 3,500. To lose one pound of weight, you need to burn off 3,500 calories per week more than you take in. To gain one pound, you have to add 3,500 calories per week more than you burn off.

The answers you give to the following two questions will determine your exact allowable calorie count.

1. How many calories does your body burn in a day?
2. How many more calories are you burning off through exercise?

Figuring out the answer will require a little math. Just like the other math problems, you can get the answer to this question online. Visit www.DietisDead.com and click on "All About YOU."

 If you want to do it here, it can all be done with a calculator. In fact, all you have to do is sit down, relax, maybe take off your shoes and socks to stretch your toes. Now take a deep breath. That's not so bad, right? You're almost ready.

Stand up, walk to the spot where you pay your bills and pick up a calculator. Now you're ready for the actual math.

The measure of how many calories you burn in a day (before exercise) is called your Resting Metabolic Rate or RMR. To figure it out you need your weight (in pounds) your height (in inches) and your age. The formula for men is first, the formula for women is next.

4 - FOR MEN - Resting Metabolic Rate

You'll need to know your weight in pounds, your height in inches and your age. Once you have those three numbers, it's time to begin. If you know something about math, the formula follows. Don't panic! If you don't know how to read the formula, we've included step-by-step instructions.

66 + (6.22 x weight in pounds) + (12.7 x height in inches) - (6.8 x age) = Resting Metabolic Rate

Perform the calculations in the parenthesis first. Then add and subtract the totals.

STEP-BY-STEP INSTRUCTIONS - Men

1. Enter the number 6.22 and MULTIPLY (x) that by your weight in pounds. Write that number beside the letter A.

   A. _____

2. Enter the number 12.7 and MULTIPLY (x) that by your height in inches. Write that number beside the letter B.

   B. _____

3. Enter the number 6.8 and MULTIPLY (x) that by your age in years. Write that number beside the letter C.

   C. _____

4. Enter 66 and ADD (+) that to the number you have beside the letter A. Write that number beside the letter D.

   D. _____

5. Enter the number beside the letter D and ADD (+) that to the number beside the letter B. Write that number beside the letter E.

   E. _____

6. Enter the number beside the letter E and SUBTRACT (-) the number beside the letter C.

   _____ - _____ = _____

   Letter E - Letter C = Resting Metabolic Rate

The answer is your Resting Metabolic Rate (RMR).

Resting Metabolic Rate = _____

4 - FOR WOMEN - Resting Metabolic Rate

You'll need to know your weight in pounds, your height in inches and your age. Once you have those three numbers, it's time to begin. If you know something about math, the formula follows. Don't panic! If you don't know how to read the formula, we've included step-by-step instructions.

655 + (4.36 x weight in pounds) + (4.32 x height in inches) - (4.7 x age) = Resting Metabolic Rate

Perform the calculations in the parenthesis first. Then add and subtract the totals.

STEP-BY-STEP INSTRUCTIONS - Women

1. Enter the number 4.36 and MULTIPLY (x) that by your weight in pounds. Write that number beside the letter A.

   A. _____

2. Enter the number 4.32 and MULTIPLY (x) that by your height in inches. Write that number beside the letter B.

   B. _____

3. Enter the number 4.7 and MULTIPLY (x) that by your age in years. Write that number beside the letter C.

   C. _____

4. Enter 655 and ADD (+) that to the number you have beside the letter A. Write that number beside the letter D.

   D. _____

5. Enter the number beside the letter D and ADD (+) that to the number beside the letter B. Write that number beside the letter E.

   E. _____

6. Enter the number beside the letter E and SUBTRACT (-) the number beside the letter C.

_____ **-** _____ **=** _____

Letter E - Letter C = Resting Metabolic Rate

The answer is your Resting Metabolic Rate (RMR).

Resting Metabolic Rate = _____

5 - How many calories do you burn from exercise?

Think about your normal week. Do you exercise? How often, and for how long? What activities do you engage in, apart from overt exercising? Take a look at the list on the next page of exercises and activities, and the number of calories they burn in 30 minutes. Your goal is to figure out how many calories you burn every day from exercise.

This list is only an example of the more common exercises. For a link to websites online that provide more information, visit www.DietisDead.com under the "Food Logs" link. You'll also find that information in calorie counting software. The caloric numbers are based on a 150 pound woman and a 180 pound man.[5]

---

5. We arrived at the calorie burned numbers by using several online "Calories Burned Calculators" and averaging them together. If you'd like to look up additional weights and exercises, the sites and direct links we used are below.

BodyBuilding.com:
  http://www.bodybuilding.com/fun/calories.htm

Health Status:
  http://www.healthstatus.com/cbc.html

WebMD Fit-o-Meter:
  http://www.webmd.com/diet/healthtool-fitness-calorie-counter

Weight Watcher Support Network – Health Discovery:
  http://www.healthdiscovery.net/links/calculators/calorie_calculator.htm

Yahoo Health:
  http://health.yahoo.com/other-other/calories-burned/healthwise--calc001.html

	150 lb. Woman	180 lb. Man
Bicycling (Light / 10 Mph or Less)	174	209
Bicycling (Moderate 11-13 Mph)	260	314
Bicycling (Vigorous 14-16 Mph)	355	427
Housework Cleaning (Heavy Cleaning)	107	129
Yardwork (Mowing Lawn with Power Mower)	176	212
Aerobic/Cardio Class (Low Intensity)	174	210
Aerobic/Cardio Class (Moderate Intensity)	219	263
Aerobic/Cardio Class (High Intensity)	279	335
Walking (Low Intensity, Slow Pace)	103	124
Walking (Medium Intensity, Moderate Pace)	131	157
Walking (High Intensity, Brisk Pace)	167	200
Running (Low Intensity, 12 Min. Per Mile)	282	338
Running (Medium Intensity, 10 Min. Per Mile)	348	418
Running (High Intensity, 8 Min. Per Mile)	441	530
Yoga	116	119
Swimming Laps (Low Intensity)	223	276
Swimming Laps (Moderate 50 Yards/Minute)	278	333
Swimming Laps (High 75 Yards/Minute)	365	438
Resistance (Weight) Training (Low Intensity)	107	129
Resistance (Weight) Training (Moderate Intensity)	165	199
Resistance (Weight) Training (High Intensity)	209	251

6 - How many calories should you eat?

 Add together your Resting Metabolic Rate and the calories you burn daily through exercise.

_____ + _____ = _____

**RMR + Calories Burned Exercising =
Total Calories Burned**

Take your total calories burned and SUBTRACT 500 if you want to lose a pound a week. ADD 500 if you want to gain a pound a week. The final number is your allowable daily calories.

_____ (+/-) _____ = _____

**Total Calories Burned (+ or -) 500 =
Allowable Daily Calories**

To lose a pound a week, you must eat 500 calories LESS than the total each day. To gain a pound a week, you must eat 500 calories MORE than the total.

This is a really critical part. You should eat AT LEAST 1,200 calories every day unless prescribed otherwise by a doctor.

Three steps to make reaching your goal easier.

First, have your Resting Metabolic Rate professionally measured with a device that measures oxygen consumption. The formula we used is good, but your actual Resting Metabolic Rate can vary by as much as 35%. An oxygen consumption test will give the precise answer. Contact your doctor, health care provider or local gym to see if they offer the RMR test.

Second, use a Heart Rate Monitor when you are doing cardio exercise to accurately measure the calories you're burning.

Third, count the number of calories in what you eat and drink. Many people count the food, but miss the extras. If you order a salad that has only 200 calories, great! But if you cover it with traditional Thousand Island Dressing (50 calories per tablespoon) and chase it with a 12 oz. can of Coca-Cola (140 calories) you more than double the calories.

On the following page is a FOOD AND DRINK LOG SHEET to help you keep track of your calories. Copy it and fill it out. Write down everything you eat and drink for two days per sheet. If you eat more or less than you should (based on your Resting Metabolic Rate and Exercise) then you need to make some changes.

You can download a full version of the food log sheet at www.DietisDead.com under the "Food Logs" link.

Software can also be used to track your food. We review several at www.DietisDead.com under the "Food Logs" link.

Food and Drink Log Sheet

Your Resting Metabolic Rate (RMR) is influenced by these factors.

Age - RMR naturally declines 2 to 3% per decade from muscle loss.

Body Composition - Pound for pound, muscles burn more calories than fat, so typically the more muscle you have, the higher it pushes your RMR.

Body Mass - People with more mass tend to have a higher RMR.

Caffeine increases RMR 3 to 7%.

Dieting - Crash diets can decrease your RMR.

Fever or Infection can increase or decrease RMR.

Gender - Men generally have higher RMR's than women because of size and body composition.

Hormones - Some hormones can increase or decrease RMR.

Meals - Small regular meals can increase your RMR.

Nicotine - Increases RMR 3 to 7%.

Ovulation - Women can have a cyclic increase in RMR of 4 to 16% during ovulation.

Pregnancy - Can increase your RMR.

Pharmaceuticals - Can increase or decrease metabolic rate.

Weather - Cold environments can increase your RMR because you expend more energy while moving around in cold weather.

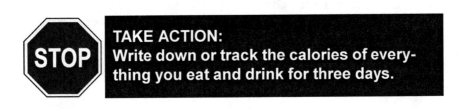

STOP

TAKE ACTION:
Write down or track the calories of everything you eat and drink for three days.

Summary
How Much Should I Eat?

Resting Metabolic Rate

The measure of how many calories you burn in a day
(before exercise) is called your Resting Metabolic Rate
or RMR. Learn your RMR to see how many calories you
really burn every day.

Calculate Exercise Calories

Once you know how many calories you burn at rest (your
RMR), you then add the calories you burn from exercise.

Calculate Daily Calorie Goals

Take your resting metabolic rate and add the number of
calories you burn daily through exercise. The number
you're left with is how many calories you need to eat
daily to maintain your weight. Add 500 more calories a
day to it and you'll gain a pound a week. Subtract 500
calories a day from it and you'll lose a pound a week.
Never go below 1,200 calories a day without a doctor's
advice!

Keep a Food and Drink Log for Three Days

In order to make a change, you have to track everything
you eat and drink so you're aware of what you're putting
in your body.

Action Items

Now you're going to learn details about food. We're going to teach you about the various types of fat, why we need fiber and what foods you can find protein in.

At the end of each chapter is an assignment. Your goal will be to look for and track things in the food you eat every day. You should track each item for three to seven days.

This is the stuff that's going to change your life. It's important you learn it.

It's not unusual for people to re-read a chapter once every day while they track something to become more familiar with the information. Do it whenever you need to refresh your memory.

The more times you read it, the better equipped you'll be to make healthy choices.

Fat

Every food you eat is a combination of three macronutrients; fat, carbohydrates and protein. This chapter will help you understand exactly what the macronutrient FAT does and how much you should include in your daily diet. Along the way we're going to bust a few myths about how healthy (or unhealthy) fat really is.

These are the essential things you need to know about fat.

> Everyone must eat some fat in their diet.
> Saturated Fats are "bad."
> Unsaturated Fats are "good."
> Trans Fats are "super bad."
> Fats substitutes may have unpleasant but interesting side effects.

Our bodies use calories for fuel much the same way cars use gas. When we eat food, our bodies burn the calories in that food and turn it into energy. A gram of fat has nine calories in it. A gram of carbohydrates or protein only have four calories each.

Fat has more than twice as many calories per gram as carbohydrates or protein. That's why small servings of fat have lots of calories. When our bodies store energy, they do so primarily in the form of fat.

Fat Technical Trivia

Fat enters your digestive system and meets with an enzyme called lipase. The lipase breaks fat into glycerol and fatty acids. These components are then reassembled into triglycerides to be transported in the bloodstream. Your muscle and fat cells absorb the triglycerides to burn as fuel or store for later use.

Do we have to eat fat?

Yes. Fat soluble vitamins require fat in order to be utilized by the body. Omega-3 and Omega-6 are considered essential fatty acids. They are "essential" because your body cannot produce them on its own and must obtain them from fat in food. They play a crucial role in brain development and normal growth. Without them you would actually starve to death.

What types of fats are there?

Saturated Fats are the "bad" fats. These fats are the primary dietary cause of high blood cholesterol which leads to heart disease. They're typically solid at room temperature.

Animal Foods with Saturated Fat - Beef, butter, cheese, cream, lamb, lard, milk (other than skim milk), pork, poultry fat, shortening and veal.

Plant Foods with Saturated Fat - Cocoa butter and tropical oils including coconut and palm oil.

Unsaturated Fats are the "good" fats. It's believed that unsaturated fats can help lower your blood cholesterol levels, but that's not an excuse to eat more of them. You should only eat them in place of saturated fats you already consume. Unsaturated fats are primarily found in oils from plants.

Unsaturated fats are broken down further into Polyunsaturated and Monounsaturated fats. **Polyunsaturated oils** are liquid at room temperature and in the refrigerator. **Monounsaturated oils** stay liquid at room temperature but start to solidify at refrigerator temperatures.

Polyunsaturated Fats - Corn, fish, flax, safflower, sesame, soybeans, sunflower seeds, nuts, seeds and their oils.[6]

Monounsaturated Fats - Avocados, nuts, canola, olive and peanut oils.[6]

---

6. Northwestern University, Nutrition Fact Sheet: Lipids; Online at: http://nuinfo-proto4.northwestern.edu/nutrition/factsheets/lipids.html; Last accessed 8/30/2010.

What are trans fatty acids or trans-fats?

These are solid fats that are created by heating liquid vegetable oils in the presence of metal catalysts and hydrogen. During the procedure some of the missing hydrogen atoms are put back into polyunsaturated fats. The process is called hydrogenation. The idea behind it was to create a food with all the cooking properties of saturated fats but the health benefits of unsaturated fats.

It didn't work. Fats that have been hydrogenated have been shown to raise blood cholesterol and are at least as bad for you as saturated fat. Margarine and vegetable shortening are examples of hydrogenated fats, and you can find it in many commercially produced baked goods and snack foods. The National Institute of Medicine has determined there are NO safe levels of trans-fats in the diet.

Technical Trivia

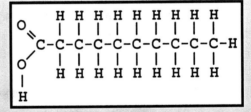

Saturated Fat

Fatty acids are molecules made up mostly of carbon and hydrogen atoms. Saturated fat (or a saturated fatty acid) has the highest possible number of hydrogen atoms attached to each carbon atom. It's "saturated" with hydrogen atoms.

Unsaturated Fat

If a fatty acid is missing a pair of hydrogen atoms in the middle of the molecule, that gap is called an "unsaturation" and the fatty acid is "monounsaturated." Mono meaning single or one. If more than one pair of hydrogen atoms are missing the fatty acid is "polyunsaturated." Poly meaning multiple or many. (The picture above is monounsaturated.)

Are there fat substitutes?

Yes. They are ingredients that mimic one or more of the roles of fat in food. According to the FDA they are grouped into two categories. Food additives and "generally recognized as safe" (GRAS) substances.

Food additives must be evaluated for safety and approved by the FDA before they can be used. Examples of food additives include carrageenan, olestra and polydextrose.

GRAS substances don't require testing before they're used in foods, typically because of the substances' long history of safe use in food. Examples of GRAS substances include dextrins, fiber, gums and starch.

Are fat substitutes safe?

The Food and Drug Administration (FDA) has ruled that any approved food additives are considered safe. But, that doesn't mean they won't hurt you. Here's the tale of one fat substitute, Olestra (Olean).

Developed by Procter & Gamble Co., Olestra adds no fat or calories to food because of it's unique chemical composition. Sounds good until you read the side effects. Foods that contained Olestra were required to carry the warning that it could cause *"...abdominal cramping and loose stools. Olestra inhibits the absorption of some vitamins and other nutrients. Vitamins A, D, E, and K have been added."* A line of potato chips was released called WOW! and the marketers went into full swing. Eat all you want without guilt! WOW!

By October, 2004 the FDA had received more than 20,000 Olestra-related reports of adverse reactions...more than any food additive in history up to that point. The reports mostly involved diarrhea, gas and cramps. All for some potato chips!

Surprisingly, Olestra was never taken off the market. By the end of 2004 WOW! Chips were rebranded and called Lays's Light, Ruffles Light,

Doritos Light, and Tostitos Light. Before you buy any food you should read the label and consider yourself warned. If you're willing to throw your stomach under the bus for potato chips, all we can say is, "Wow!"

VITAL STATISTIC 7 - How much fat should you eat?

According to the *Dietary Guidelines for Americans,* jointly issued by the United States Departments of Agriculture (USDA) and Health and Human Services, *"total fat consumption should be limited to 30 percent or less of total caloric intake, and saturated fat intake should be limited to less than 10 percent of total caloric intake."*

People who are trying to lose weight or increase muscle, should consider decreasing total fat to approximately 25% of total calories. Individuals with heart problems, or a family history of coronary diseases should consider reducing total fat to 20% or less of total calories. If you want to skip the math, go to wwwDietisDead.com under "All About YOU" and we'll figure it out for you.

 Take the allowable daily calories you calculated on page 45 or 46 and multiply that by the percentage of fat you should take in.

30% USDA Maximum Fat Percentage
25% Maximum Fat Percentage if you're trying to lose weight or build muscle.
20% Maximum Fat Percentage if you have heart problems or a family history of coronary heart disease.

Then take the answer and divide it by 9 to get your total fat grams daily.

_____ **X** _____ **=** _____
**Allowable Daily Calories x Maximum Fat Percentage
= Total Fat Calories**

_____ **÷ 9 =** _____
Total Fat Calories ÷ 9 = Total Fat Grams Daily

Simply reducing the amount of fat you eat will not help you lose weight. Just look at what's happened to Americans since the 1960s.

In 1971, the number of people in the United States that were classified as obese was 14.5%. That number slowly crept up and by the year 2000, 30.9% of Americans were considered obese according to the Centers for Disease Control (CDC).[7]

Ironically that happened as the consumption of fat dropped. From the late 1950s to the mid 1960s Americans took in 40-42% of their total calories from fat.[8] As the dangers of certain types of fat became known, the percentage of fat that people ate in their diet declined.

The amount of fat we were eating went down, but the levels of obesity more than doubled. Americans cut the fat but we haven't cut the calories. Most of those calorie increases have come from carbohydrates. We'll tell you more about that in the next chapter.

7. JD Wright, MPH, J Kennedy-Stephenson, MS, CY Wang, PhD, MA McDowell, MPH, CL Johnson, MSPH, National Center for Health Statistics, CDC. *Trends in Intake of Energy and Macronutrients --- United States, 1971--2000* Morbidity and Mortality Weekly Report (MMWR), February 6, 2004 / 53(04);80-82

8. AM Stephen and NJ Wald, Division of Nutrition and Dietetics, College of Pharmacy, University of Saskatchewan Saskatton, Canada. *Trends in individual consumption of dietary fat in the United States, 1920-1984* American Journal of Clinical Nutrition, Vol 52, 457-469

 TAKE ACTION:
Write down what types and how many grams of fat you eat for at least three days.

Summary
Fat

Fat is Important

Everyone has to eat some fat in their diet.

Saturated Fats are "Bad"

Saturated fats are the primary dietary cause of high blood cholesterol which leads to heart disease. They're typically solid at room temperature.

Unsaturated Fats are "Good"

Unsaturated fats can help lower your blood cholesterol levels. They're usually liquid at room temperature.

Trans-Fats are "SuperBad"

The National Institute of Medicine has determined there are NO safe levels of trans-fats in the diet.

Fat Substitutes can be a Problem

Fat substitutes like Olestra/Olean may cause interesting and unpleasant side effects.

Track Your Fat for at Least Three Days

Work on keeping your fat intake below 30% of your total calories.

Carbohydrates

Once upon a time the world's health nuts and fitness gurus were fighting the war on fat. We were lectured about the ills of too much fat in our diets and the United States Department of Argiculture Food Pyramid clearly depicted that fat should be the smallest portion of our daily food intake. We had Susan Powter and her woman-power infomercials screaming *"It's fat that makes you fat!"* and we saw our grocery aisles fill up with fat free cookies, chips and snacks. Then, along came the mid 1990s when the newest REAL enemy was revealed: Carbohydrates (or carbs).

The low carb craze was huge. From *Atkins*, to *South Beach, Sugar Busters* to *The Zone*, we were bombarded with experts telling us that now, carbohydrates were the reason we were fat.

Were they right? Was it the carbohydrates that were the bane of dieters everywhere? All this time spent beating fat like the proverbial rented mule, blaming it for society's burgeoning, bloated ills, and now there's a new culprit? By deductive reasoning, will that pesky protein be blamed next? Let's explore this love-hate relationship with carbohydrates and to quote Susan Powter, *"Stop the Insanity!"*

These are the essential things you need to know about carbohydrates.

Carbs are your bodies preferred source of energy.
Simple carbs provide a quick release of energy.
Complex carbs give a more long lasting and sustained energy release.
Resistant starches are a carb that seem to have health benefits.
"Net Carb" labels mean nothing with no industry-common standard.

What are carbohydrates?

Carbohydrates are your body's preferred source of fuel. They provide most of the energy we need for the little things that mean so much; like heartbeat, digestion and breathing.

How does your body turn carbs into energy?

Your body breaks all carbs down to sugar, or glucose, which then fuel your cells. The speed at which foods break down is represented on a scale called the glycemic index.

High Glycemic Index Carbohydrates have little or no fiber, break down rapidly and are quickly converted to energy.

Low Glycemic Index Carbohydrates are trapped in fiber, take much longer to break down and are converted, much more slowly, to energy.

If you're looking for a quick burst of energy, eat foods higher on the glycemic index. If you want more sustained energy, choose low glycemic index foods.

Watch Your Blood Sugar

There are some people who should monitor the glycemic index of foods. Diabetics are taught to monitor the glycemic index to prevent dangerous spikes in blood sugar levels. There is also evidence that foods with a low glycemic index provide beneficial effects for people with ischemic heart disease.

Find out if the foods you eat are higher or lower on the glycemic index. For a database with the Glycemic Index of foods visit www.glycemicindex.com.

Are there different types of carbs?

On a very basic level, carbs can be divided into two categories: Simple Carbs and Complex Carbs.

Simple carbs are two molecule sugars that act to provide quick energy when your body digests them. A simple carb provides fuel for your body for 30 to 60 minutes.

Simple Carb Foods include: Bananas, French Fries, Honey, Potatoes, Soft Drinks, Sugar (Brown, Raw or White), White Bread, White Pasta and White Rice.

Complex carbs are long chains of glucose that provide a slow release of energy when digested. A complex carb provides fuel for your body for three to four hours.

Complex Carb Foods include: Bulgar, Barley, Beans, Bran, Brown Rice, Couscous, Legumes, Oats, Non-starchy Vegetables, Whole Fruits, Whole Grain Breakfast Cereals, Whole Wheat and Yams.

There is a third type of carbohydrate that we don't often hear about. It is somewhat of a "magic" carb that is relatively easy to find and you may already be eating them and not even realize their healthy benefits. It's called resistant starch.

Resistant Starch is a type of carbohydrate that digests so slowly, it goes through the small intestine without being digested. It "resists" digestion. Here's how it works.

When you eat a resistant starch, it's bulky and takes up space in your digestive system, this makes you feel full. Because your small intestine doesn't absorb or digest it, your body doesn't turn the excess you eat into fat. As it enters the large intestine your body ferments it. One of the byproducts of resistant starch fermentation is the creation of a fatty acid called butyrate, which blocks the body's ability to burn carbohydrates. Carbohydrates are the body's preferred source of fuel. So when butyrate blocks your ability to burn carbs, your body looks for fat to burn instead.

A study at the University of Colorado Health Sciences Center found that replacing just 5.4% of daily carb intake with resistant starch increases fat burning by an astonishing 23%.[9]

The benefits of butyrate don't stop there. Research now indicates the butyrate produced by resistant starch may also protect the lining of the colon. It helps boost the absorption of calcium, blocks the absorption of cancer-causing substances and makes the colon less vulnerable to deoxyribonucleic (DNA) damage.[10]

Diabetics that eat resistant starch benefit because it doesn't raise blood sugar or insulin levels. Lower blood sugar means more energy and arteries that aren't hardening or getting clogged. A study conducted at the Institute of Nutrition and Food Safety in Beijing showed resistant starch can even improve insulin resistance in patients with type 2 diabetes.[11]

To get more in your diet, you should know there are at least four types of resistant starch. Here they are.

---

9. Higgins JA, Higbee DR, Donahoo WT, Brown IL, Bell ML, Bessesen DH. *Resistant starch consumption promotes lipid oxidation*. From the University of Colorado Health Sciences Center, Center for Human Nutrition, Denver, Colorado 80262, USA. Higgins.Janine@tchden.org. Nutr Metab (Lond). 2004 Oct 6;1(1):8.

10. Nofrarías M, Martínez-Puig D, Pujols J, Majó N, Pérez JF. *Resistant starch consumption promotes lipid oxidation*. From the Centre de Recerca en Sanitat Animal, Departament de Sanitat i d'Anatomia Animals, Universitat Autònoma de Barcelona, Bellaterra, Spain. miquel.nofrarias@cresa.uab.cat. Nutrition. 2007 Nov-Dec;23(11-12):861-70.

11. Zhang WQ, Wang HW, Zhang YM, Yang YX. *Long-term intake of resistant starch improves colonic mucosal integrity and reduces gut apoptosis and blood immune cells*. From the Institute of Nutrition and Food Safety, Chinese Center for Disease Control and Prevention, Beijing 100050, China. Zhonghua Yu Fang Yi Xue Za Zhi. 2007 Mar;41(2):101-4.

Resistant Starch 1 [RS1]

Barley, whole grains, brown rice, beans and legumes cooked intact are one type. The fibrous "shell" makes it difficult for the small intestines to break down. If you can avoid it, don't mix beans with products like Bean-o. While Bean-o increases the digestibility of beans, it decreases the amount of resistant starch.

Resistant Starch 2 [RS2]

Slightly green bananas, plantains, high-amylose corn and raw potatoes are a second type. They have a chemical structure that digestive enzymes can't break down.

Resistant Starch 3 [RS3]

The third type are a few starchy foods that are cooled before eating. When some starchy foods are cooked, the starch absorbs water and swells. As it cools, a portion of the starch crystallizes into resistant starch. Potatoes (like those in a potato salad) and rice (rice pudding) are two examples. The only caveat is you can't re-heat that food or the crystalline structure breaks down and the levels of resistant starch drop dramatically.

Resistant Starch 4 [RS4]

The fourth type of resistant starch is made synthetically. It is unclear if artificially made resistant starches have the same beneficial effects the other three types have, so you may want to avoid them until more research has been done.

What are "Net Carbs" or "Net Atkins Count"?

Marketing gimmicks. The premise of many low carb diets is that if you don't have easily metabolized carbohydrates available, your body will use stored fats for energy. Foods with low "Net Carb" or "Net Atkins Count" are supposedly acceptable, even if their overall carb count is higher, because the carbs come from artificial sweeteners and fiber. Theoretically the fiber will help you feel "full" longer, stopping you from overeating.

Research does not back up the claims. There is no Food and Drug Administration (FDA) regulation of the term "Net Carb" or "Net Atkins Count" to verify a products' claim. If you're trying to lose weight, you should pay more attention to the total calories than any claims of "Net Carbs" or "Net Atkins Count." People who have lost weight on low carb diets have done so because the total number of daily calories consumed was reduced.

Some of these diets are not only gimmicks but are unhealthy. A low carb diet for, say... a diabetic would still call for 45% of daily calories from carbohydrates. A modest dietary intake of 1500 calories still calls for 168 grams of carbohydrates.

A diet such as Atkins recommends only 40 to 60 grams of carbohydrates a day.[12] This is far too low. The notion that one can exchange carbohydrates with bacon, eggs and bun-less cheeseburgers is simply bad science. With side effects like lethargy, depression, constipation and clogged arteries, no nutritionist in their right mind would endorse a diet so high in saturated fat and so dangerously low in carbohydrates.

---

12. Robert C. Atkins. *Dr. Atkins' New Diet Revolution, Revised Edition*. M.Evans; 3 Sub edition (September 25, 2003)

TAKE ACTION:
For the next week, reduce simple carbs from your diet and replace them with complex carbs and resistant starches.

Summary
Carbohydrates

Carbs Provide Energy

Carbs are your bodies preferred source of energy.

Simple Carbs

Simple carbs provide a quick release of energy. These are best consumed first thing in the morning and right after a workout.

Complex Carbs

Complex carbs give a more long lasting and sustained energy release.

Resistant Starch

Resistant starches are a carb that seem to have health benefits.

Net Carbs

"Net Carb" labels mean nothing because there is no common standard.

Sugar

Sugar is a carbohydrate. The reason we're giving it a chapter of it's own is because of all the misconceptions surrounding it.

These are the essential things you need to know about sugar.

Most sugars are simple carbs.
Sugars are hiding in thousands of food and drink items.
Sugars should make up no more than 6-10% of your total calories.

Pop Quiz! What do the following things have in common?

White Sugar	Brown Sugar	Raw Sugar
Natural Sugar	Powdered Sugar	Corn Syrup
Molasses	Maple Syrup	Honey

When comparing equal serving sizes, they all have nearly the same amount of one basic component...sugar.

Take a look at the labels: 1 tablespoon of raw sugar has 12 grams of sugar. 1 tablespoon of maple syrup has 12 grams of sugar. 1 tablespoon of corn syrup has 12 grams of sugar. Are you beginning to see a pattern here? Dress it up any way you want, they're all sugar.

"That doesn't matter" you may say, "I eat raw sugar/honey/pure cane sugar because it's NATURAL and that's better for me!" Sorry folks, if you're saying that, you're a sucker for good marketing. The element that makes all those products sweet is sucrose, and no matter what form your sucrose comes in, when you eat it it's all absorbed and processed by your body exactly the same way. That's where the problem lies.

Americans are eating more than three times as much sugar as they should and it's hidden in thousands of everyday foods. People expect to find sugar in breakfast cereals and pancakes, but did you know sugar is added to ketchup, bread and soups? Instant oatmeal, yogurt and even cheeses are loaded with sugar.

One of the reasons we're seeing so much sugar in foods today is because in the 1970s fat was targeted as a public health menace. Over the years companies reformulated thousands of products to replace their fat with sugars. At the same time the food industry began increasing its use of high-fructose corn syrup, a cheap and tasty man-made sugar.

We picked up food labels and got excited when companies made them FAT FREE. What we failed to realize was that many products simply swapped out FAT for SUGAR. The calorie counts never changed.

Sugar is everywhere.

These are the names you can find sugar hiding under on a food label.

Corn Syrup - Crystalline Fructos - Dextrose - Fructose - Fruit Juice Concentrates - Glucose - High-Fructose Corn Syrup - High-Maltose Corn Syrup - Honey - Honey Lactose - Invert Sugar - Lactose - Malt - Maltose - Molasses - Sucrose - Syrup

To understand what excess sugar is doing to our bodies, it's important to understand how it goes through our bodies.

When we eat carbohydrates our bodies convert the carbs into glucose, or blood sugar. The glucose gives us energy. Refined carbohydrates such as white rice, flour and sugar turn into glucose faster than unrefined whole grain foods, because the harder to digest fibrous outer shells from whole grains are removed.

When your body gets higher levels of glucose (from the refined carbs) it pumps out more insulin, a hormone that moderates sugar levels in the bloodstream. Unfortunately, for many people the insulin then drives the blood sugar too low, leaving you feeling hungry and tired.

High fructose corn syrup (HFCS) reality check.

It's been demonized as the "unhealthiest sugar ever created." But don't worry, it's mostly hysteria and just a little science. These are the facts.

When ordinary sugar (sucrose) breaks down in your body, it turns into 50% fructose and 50% glucose. When HFCS breaks down it turns into 55% fructose and 45% glucose. Virtually the same.

The reason it's become an issue is because researchers believe the higher the fructose content, the greater the potential for health problems. There's a lot of speculation, but as of January 2010 not a single definitive study on humans show that HFCS is conclusively worse than regular sugar.[13]

Don't bother switching from one type of sugar to another if you're trying to be healthier. The best option is to simply reduce your intake from ALL sources of sugar.

VITAL STATISTIC 8 - How much sugar should you eat?

Sugar is such a politically charged issue even the United States Department of Agriculture has avoided giving recommendations. For a reliable number we have to refer to the World Health Organization (WHO). They state that a healthy person should get no more than 6-10% of their total calories from sugar.[14]

---

13. Tappy L, Lê KA. *Metabolic effects of fructose and the worldwide increase in obesity*. From the Department of Physiology, Faculty of Biology and Medicine, University of Lausanne, CH-1005 Lausanne, Switzerland. luc.tappy@unil.ch.Physiol Rev. 2010 Jan;90(1):23-46

14. N.P. Steyn, N.G. Myburgh, & J.H. Nel. *Evidence to support a food-based dietary guideline on sugar consumption in South Africa*. From the Bulletin of the World Health Organization (BLT). POLICY AND PRACTICE, Volume 81, Number 8, 2003, 551-628

That works out to between 40 and 55 grams per person eating a 2,000 calorie a day diet. If you're eating fewer calories, you should take in less sugar. If you're eating more calories, you can take in more sugar. Here's how to calculate it for yourself.

Remember, we'll calculate it for you online at www.DietisDead.com under the "All About YOU" link.

 Take the allowable daily calories you calculated on page 48 and multiply that by 10%. Then take the answer and divide it by 4 to get your total sugar grams daily.

_____ **X** _____ **% =** _____
Allowable Daily Calories x 10% = Total Sugar Calories

_____ **÷ 4 =** _____
Total Sugar Calories ÷ 4 = Total Sugar Grams Daily

For three days you need to record your sugar intake. The first day you should simply count how many grams of sugar you're eating. If it's too high, you goal for the next two days is to try and take in less. If you're too low, you may want to consider foods with a higher sugar content. Following are strategies to reduce your sugar.

Five Steps to Reduce Sugar in Your Diet

1. Choose Complex Carbohydrates.

Walter Willett, M.D. and professor of nutrition at the Harvard School of Public Health suggests we eat more "Coarsely ground or intact grains [because they] have a slow, low and steady effect on blood sugar and insulin levels."

Complex Carb Foods include: Bulgar, Barley, Beans, Bran, Brown Rice, Couscous, Legumes, Oats, Non-starchy Vegetables, Whole Fruits, Whole Grain Breakfast Cereals, Whole Wheat and Yams.

2. Don't eat carbs alone.

Simple carbs breakdown into glucose rather rapidly. Mix them with fat or protein and it will be absorbed into the bloodstream more slowly, helping prevent sudden spikes in your insulin levels.

Eat an apple, but put some peanut butter on it. Don't choose regular pasta and tomato sauce; try whole-wheat pasta with meat sauce. Keep in mind you may have to reduce your carbs when you combine, you shouldn't simply pile on additional calories.

3. Use more spices.

These will help you get over your carb withdrawal. Try wasabi or salsas. Add lemon or lime zest to salads and green vegetables. Olive oil is wonderful on morning toast in place of jelly.

4. Read food labels.

If sugar (or high-fructose corn syrup) is the first or second ingredient, look for alternatives. When each serving on the label has more than 5 or 10 grams of sugar in it, you should look for a replacement.

Labels that scream "fat free" aren't necessarily healthy. In many cases the fat has been replaced with sugar. Some food "low-fat" versions are better for you than their "fat free" alternatives. Compare the nutritional labels.

5. Don't be afraid of the substitutes.

Sweet'N Low, Equal and Splenda are sensible options and you can now get versions of them to cook with. Depending on how they're used, they taste good and won't spike your blood sugar. Just remember the basics.

Artificial sweeteners are (for the most part) safe. In the 1980s there were references to studies that showed the main ingredient in Sweet'N Low, saccharin, was linked to cancer. Later studies rebuked that claim when it was revealed that humans would have to consume enormous quantities to approach the levels given to lab rats. Further research has now shown that almost anything can be cancerous if given in the amounts originally administered in the saccharin study.

Obesity is far more damaging to the health of most people than any theoretical risks these sugar replacements may pose.

If you don't like the taste of a particular artificial sweetener, experiment. If Equal has a metallic taste and Sweet'N Low is too bitter, try combing one of each in your drink. Still not working for you? Try Splenda, Stevia or one of the artificial sweeteners with a little real sugar.

Don't expect to lose weight just because you've cut down on sugar. You have to reduce the total calories you're consuming, not just the sugars. A sugar free snack is not an excuse to binge.

Cutting down on simple sugars isn't a magic bullet to better health. But, if you try and follow these suggestions and limit your intake according to the World Health Organization recommendations, approximately 40 to 55 grams of sugar per person per day, you'll be taking a giant step toward better health.

TAKE ACTION:
Over the next seven days, count how many grams of sugar you're eating and try to keep it at 10% of your total calories or less.

Summary
Sugar

Sugar

Most sugars are simple carbs.

Where is Sugar

Sugars are hiding in thousands of food and drink items.

How Much Sugar

Sugars should make up no more than 6-10% of your total calories. An easy way to calculate is make sure there is 1 gram of sugar (or less) for every 40 calories you eat.

Track Your Sugar for a Week

Try to keep your total sugar intake at 10% or less of your total calories.

Protein

Protein provides the structure for all living things. After water, protein accounts for the greatest portion of human body weight. A typical person is 60% water, 20% protein and most of the rest minerals (like calcium in bones). But that's not all. Protein's also a transport carrier, collagen for supportive tissue, enzymes to help with chemical reactions like digestion and antibodies for immune defense .

These are the essential things you need to know about protein.

Proteins are a chain of amino acids.
Your body uses protein to repair and build up muscle.
Protein is found in both meats and vegetables, but is typically higher in meats.
There is no evidence that taking protein supplements are any better or worse than getting protein from the food you eat.

Protein helps with all sorts of bodily functions. But, protein isn't marketed for its ability to aid digestion or immune defense. It's sold with the promise that if you eat it, you'll build more muscle. Just squeeze open a couple of cans of protein-rich spinach, and you'll immediately get rippling muscles, and be able to save the day.

Unfortunately, extra protein alone does not help build more muscle. Drinking a protein shake every day won't make you stronger. It's all about exercise. Exercise COMBINED with an appropriate intake of protein can help you build muscle.

The amount of protein you should take in varies by the type of exercises you do and your diet. We'll tell you on the next page how to calculate it, or have us do it for you at www.DietisDead.com under "All About YOU."

Protein Technical Trivia

What is Protein?

All proteins are a chain of amino acids. An amino acid is a small molecule that acts as the building block of any cell. That's it. But, there are a lot of different amino acids, and they're broken down into ESSENTIAL and NON-ESSENTIAL.

Here's what that means.

The essential amino acids cannot be created so the only way to get them is through food. **There are Nine Essential Amino Acids:**

L-Isoleucine, Leucine, Lysine, Methionine, Phenylalanine, Threonine, Tryptophan, Valine and Histidine.

(We consider histidine to be an essential amino acid because of the problems with haemoglobin concentrations that occur when people are on a histidine-free diet.)

A non-essential amino acid is one your body can create out of other chemicals in your body.

Non-Essential Amino Acids are Alanine, Asparagine, Aspartic Acid, Citrulline, Cystine and Glutamate.

We've added a third group that we call, conditionally essential amino acids. A conditionally essential amino acid is one that must be supplied from outside sources to people who are unable to synthesize it in adequate amounts.

Conditionally essential amino acids are Arginine, Cysteine, Glycine, Glutamine, Proline, Serine and Tyrosine.

VITAL STATISTIC 9 - How much protein should you eat?

1 The <u>Reference Daily Intake</u> set by the <u>Food and Nutrition Board</u> for protein is **<u>0.32 grams of protein per pound of body weight</u>**. That means a 180 pound person would need to take in about 58 grams of protein every day.[15] But that's not the final word.

2 <u>**ENDURANCE TRAINING**</u> (running, jogging, swimming, biking, etc.) can dramatically increase the required amounts. **<u>.55 to .64 grams of protein per pound</u>** of bodyweight per day. So now that 180 pound person should take in 99 to 115 grams of protein every day.

3 <u>**STRENGTH TRAINING**</u> (moving weights) bumps it up even further. **<u>.73 to .78 grams of protein per pound</u>** of bodyweight per day. In this category that 180 pound person would need 131 to 140 grams of protein each day.

If you're a **<u>VEGETARIAN</u>** it is suggested you **increase your protein intake above suggested levels by another 10%**. The increase is because plant proteins are considered lower quality and they don't have as many of the essential amino acids that animal proteins do. The 10% increase is to make up for those deficiencies. (There is one exception. Soy protein does contain all the essential amino acids.)

<u>**PREGNANT WOMEN**</u> generally need an **<u>extra 10 grams of protein per day</u>** above suggested levels.

<u>**WOMEN WHO ARE NURSING**</u> typically need **<u>15 grams a day extra the first 6 months</u>**, dropping to **<u>12 grams a day extra the second six months</u>**.

---

15. Joanne R. Lupton et al. *Dietary Reference Intakes Energy, Carbohydrate, Fiber, Fat, Fatty Acids, Cholesterol, Protein, and Amino Acids*. From the Food and Nutrition Board, Institute of Medicine of the National Academies, THE NATIONAL ACADEMIES PRESS 500 Fifth Street, N.W. Washington, DC 20001: Copyright 2002/2005; Page 1330.

Supplement companies suggest much higher levels of protein consumption, from 1 to 2 grams of protein per pound of bodyweight per day. Unfortunately, these higher levels are based on anecdotal evidence and not controlled clinical trials.

Here's how to calculate how much protein YOU should take in daily. Remember, we'll figure this out for you online at www.DietisDead.com.

Choose 1 (Basic), 2 (Endurance) or 3 (Strength) from the previous page and multiply that by how many pounds you weigh. The answer is how many grams of protein you should eat in a day.

X _____ **=** _____
Choose 1, 2 or 3 x Pounds = Grams of Protein

If you're a vegan, vegetarian, pregnant or nursing you'll need to increase that number. And, if you're a nursing vegetarian in strength training, you'll have to eat so many vegetables, you may want to consider investing in spinach futures.

Vegan or Vegetarian

_____ **X   110% =** _____
Total Grams of Protein x 110% = Vegan Grams of Protein

Pregnant

_____ **+   10 =** _____
Total Grams of Protein + 10 = Pregnant Grams of Protein

Nursing First Six Months

_____ **+   15 =** _____
Total Grams of Protein + 15 = Nursing Grams of Protein

Nursing Second Six Months

_____ +   12 = _____
Total Grams of Protein + 12 = Nursing Grams of Protein

How much protein is too much?

The Food and Nutrition Board of the Institute of Medicine suggest that if more than 35% of your total daily calories are protein, you're probably eating too much.[16] Excess protein can't be stored in the body (like fat and carbs) so eating too much may put a strain on the kidneys and liver.

What foods have protein in them?

We get protein from animal and vegetable sources. Animal sources are typically considered "complete proteins" because they contain all of the essential amino acids.

Animal Proteins can be found in: Eggs, Fish, Meat and Milk.

Vegetables do contain protein, but most are lower than meats or missing some of the essential amino acids. The only vegetable protein source that has all the essential amino acids is soy. If you're a vegan or vegetarian the key is combining different foods so you can get all the essential amino acids required daily.

Vegetable Proteins can be found in: Beans, Nuts and Soybeans.

---

16. Joanne R. Lupton et al. _Dietary Reference Intakes Energy, Carbohydrate, Fiber, Fat, Fatty Acids, Cholesterol, Protein, and Amino Acids_. From the Food and Nutrition Board, Institute of Medicine of the National Academies, THE NATIONAL ACADEMIES PRESS 500 Fifth Street, N.W. Washington, DC 20001: Copyright 2002/2005; Page 589.

Following are 15 foods that contain protein, and approximately how many grams of protein each serving has. This list to to give you an idea of how much protein you can expect to find in some common foods.

Protein content for common food items.

	Calories	Grams of Protein
Whole Wheat Bread (2 Slices)	200	8
Green Beans (10 Beans / 1.9 oz.)	17	1
Broccoli (6 Florets / 5 oz.)	48	4
Chicken Grilled (1 Breast / 4 oz.)	124	26.1
Yogurt (1 Cup / 8.6 oz.)	250	10.7
Cheese Fat Free (2 Slices / 1.4 oz.)	62	9.5
Canned Tuna Fish (2 oz. Low Sodium)	60	13
Snapper Fish Baked (4 oz.)	147	29.7
Kidney Beans (1/2 Cup / 6.2 oz.)	112	7.7
Almonds Raw (1/4 Cup)	207	7.6
Beef (4 oz. Sirloin)	212	34.2
Milk Fat Free (1 Cup)	91	8.7
Tofu Firm (1/4 Block / 2.9 oz.)	117	12.8
Egg White (1 Egg)	17	3.6
Whole Egg (1 Egg)	78	6.3

TAKE ACTION:
Over the next seven days, count how many grams of protein you're eating and make sure it's enough.

Summary
Protein

What is Protein

Proteins are chains of amino acids.

Why do we Need Protein

Your body uses protein to repair and build up muscle, plus numerous other essential functions.

What Foods Have Protein

Protein is found in both meats and vegetables, but is typically higher in meats.

Protein Supplements

There is no evidence that taking protein supplements are any better or worse than getting protein from the food you eat.

Track Your Protein for a Week

Write down how many grams of protein you eat every day and see if you're meeting the minimum requirements.

Protein From Supplements - *A Shopping Guide*

This information is for those of you who are buying protein supplements because you're unwilling or unable to get enough from your diet. Think of it as a guide to decipher what the labels are saying. <u>If you don't buy protein supplements, feel free to skip this chapter.</u>

Supplements primarily get their protein from five places. Here's where they come from, along with their good and bad points.

EGG

<u>Egg (Ovalbumen) protein is from egg whites</u>. This was long considered the best source of protein for supplements because of its excellent amino acid profile. However, since the 1990s supplement companies have significantly improved their other products and now whey protein is considered the best.

<u>Whole Egg protein</u> has many of the same attributes of egg white protein, but with extra calories and fat.

SOY

<u>Soy is the highest quality vegetable protein</u> and is extracted from soybeans. It has also been shown to enhance fat loss more effectively than casein and may help reduce cholesterol levels.

Dairy (Casein and Whey)

<u>Casein protein</u> makes up about 80% of the protein in milk. When milk is curdled the casein represents the curd. Casein is called a slow protein

because it's digested more slowly. This high quality protein is great for meals throughout the day. Casein is also used at night to slow the rate at which muscles break down (known as catabolism) while sleeping.

Whey protein makes up about 20% of the protein in milk. When milk is curdled the whey ends up as a separate liquid. Whey protein is called a fast protein because it's digested rapidly. Whey protein is recommended first thing in the morning, after exercise or anytime you need a quick burst of amino acids because of its rapid uptake. Whey protein may help increase levels of glutathione (GSH), a significant antioxidant-fighting mechanism.

This is what the labels mean.

In an effort to convince you that THEIR protein supplement is superior, companies list several claims on the label. Most of those claims describe either how protein is extracted from the source or processed afterwards. Here is a list of the major extraction and processing methods along with their purported benefits. You don't need to read this now, use this before you buy protein to understand what all the marketing claims mean.

Extraction Methods

Calcium/Sodium/Potassium Caseinate - Protein is extracted from casein through acidification with alkaline substances like calcium, sodium or potassium. Avoid Sodium Caseinate if you're trying to cut sodium levels and look for Calcium Caseinate if you need more calcium.

Hydrolyzed Casein Protein - Casein protein that is broken down into simpler compounds by a reaction with water. These proteins are shorter, require less digestion in the stomach and are digested more rapidly that other casein proteins.

Micellar Casein - Microfiltration is the process used to separate the casein portion of milk from the lactose, fat and whey. Micellar Casein isn't denatured (meaning not altered or treated with heat or acid). It is the slowest digesting of the casein proteins.

Micronparticulated Whey Protein - Through micronization of the whey protein the protein particle size is reduced by one-fifth. That creates a greater surface area to volume meaning it mixes well with shakes and increases the speed of digestion. This is a very fast digesting protein, even faster than whey protein isolate.

Milk Protein Concentrate - Typically produced through ultrafiltration, this has a protein content around 80% and contains both the whey and casein fractions of milk.

Milk Protein Isolate - A product of both casein and whey products extracted through an ultra filtration process. The protein content can be 85% or higher.

Soy Protein Concentrate - Soybean flour or flakes are put through an extraction process with water or alcohol to remove some of the carbs. The protein content is typically 65%. It often contains indigestible carbs that can cause gas in some people.

Soy Protein Isolate - Soy concentrate is processed further to remove most of the gas producing carbs and fats for a product that is often higher than 90% protein. It is digested slower than whey, but faster than casein.

Whey Protein Concentrate - Through ultrafiltration and microfiltration, microscopic filters are used to physically separate the protein from fat, carbohydrates, lactose and other materials in milk. It can be higher in fat and lactose so may not be the best choice for anyone dieting or lactose intolerant. This can be sourced at 70%-80% protein per final product.

Whey Protein Hydrolysate - This is Whey Protein Isolate taken through one additional step. Enzymes break down (hydrolyze) the protein making short chains of amino acids. This is the fastest absorbing of the whey proteins.

Whey Protein Isolate - Take Whey Protein Concentrate and process it further through longer filtering or ion exchange and you end up with Whey

Protein Isolate. This is typically very low in fat and lactose, so it's good for people who are lactose intolerant. The protein content is 90% or higher.

Whey Protein Isolate Cold Filtration - Proteins are separated through the use of micro filtering in a cold environment. The reason for the chilling is to preserve the undenatured proteins. (Undenatured means - To prevent the tertiary structure of a protein from unfolding, so that its original properties, especially its biological activity, aren't diminished or eliminated.) This can be sourced at 35%-80% protein per final product.

Whey Protein Isolate Ion Exchange - In a process called ion exchange, milk is put through a static electrical charge separating the whey from lactose and fat. This can be sourced as high as 96% protein.

Whey Protein Isolate Microfiltration - Whey protein concentrate taken one step further by separating the proteins using natural ceramic filters. This is typically very low in fat and lactose, so it's good for people who are lactose intolerant. This can be sourced up to 92% protein per final product.

Whole Milk Protein - The protein is extracted through filtration to remove much of the carbs and fat.

Protein Processing Methods

Cross-Flow Microfiltration - Whey protein is separated from fat and lactose with ceramic filters in a low temperature process. (This is the same process as Microfiltration, see below.)

Hydrolysis - This is a process where protein is predigested or broken down into peptides (small chains of amino acids). The theory is that it helps you absorb the protein more efficiently. We emphasize that it's a theory, because it's based on a study where the protein was supplied to patients' intestines via a tube. Proteins marketing themselves as superior because of this process lack clinical proof.

Ion Exchange - Ionically charged resins and chemicals such as hydrochloric acid and sodium hydroxide are used to separate protein.

Microfiltration - Whey protein is separated from fat and lactose with ceramic filters in a low temperature process. (This is the same process as Cross-Flow Microfiltration, see above.)

Ultrafiltration - Pressure and a porous membrane are used to separate the fat and lactose from milk proteins.

The Bottom Line

There is a raging debate going on about what protein source is "better" for bodybuilders. We choose not to pick any protein over any other simply because the research is not conclusive. Until long-term clinical trials are conducted, we suggest you consume proteins from all the major sources. Don't be taken in by the supplement company "advertorials."

We would also like to point out there is no research proving that protein supplements are any better than eating protein rich foods. Taking protein supplements are a matter of convenience when protein laden foods are unavailable, inconvenient or to boost protein calories without a corresponding increase in fat and carbohydrates.

Fiber

A common introduction to the concept of "adding fiber" is the television commercial with grandpa mixing, like an unimaginative mad scientist, an Einstein frightwig sort of genius, concocting a simple cloudy liquid at the breakfast nook.

Back in the early days of fiber supplements, the liquid simply turned a chalky color to let the unfortunate partaker know it was ready, like it was just waiting for a few final ingredients before it became cement. When grandpa drank it, he closed his eyes, wrinkled up his nose, and contorted his face into a sort of grimace, as if the fiber he was ingesting were liquefied strands from a shipment meant for the underwear factory.

Why go through with it? Why devote time and energy to drinking something that tastes like rotted cardboard? For years doctors have been saying the health benefits of supplemental fiber far outweigh the momentary discomfort. It turns out, the doctors were right.

These are the essential things you need to know about fiber.

> Fiber can reduce the risk of coronary heart disease by 40%.
> People with higher cereal fiber diets have a lower risk of type 2 diabetes.
> Fiber can help reduce the incidence of diverticular disease.
> Fiber can help prevent obesity.

Fiber - The Bad News

Contrary to popular belief, adding fiber to your diet does NOT seem to be able to protect against colorectal cancer.

Over the years there were small studies that seemed to show some promise, but then came the "Nurses Study" conducted by the Department of Medicine, Brigham and Women's Hospital and Harvard Medical School.

More than 76,000 women were followed for 16 years. The result? 76,000 stalking complaints. Not really, but here's what they found.

"After adjustment for age, established risk factors, and total energy intake, we found no association between the intake of dietary fiber and the risk of colorectal cancer..."[17] It was a big blow to cancer researchers hoping that fiber might help them in their fight.

The news is also bad for fiber and its supposed "cholesterol lowering" abilities.

The Department of Nutrition at the Harvard School of Public Health looked into 67 dietary fiber trials before concluding the cholesterol lowering effect of fiber is *"small within the practical range of intake"* and that *"increasing soluble fiber can make only a small contribution to dietary therapy to lower cholesterol."*[18] Eating more fiber wasn't going to reduce cholesterol in any significant way.

Remember, when you're reading food labels making claims about their ability to reduce cholesterol, it's mostly marketing hype. They're trying to convince you to buy something that may, or may not, leave your tongue feeling like it's covered in tree bark. Now for the good news.

Fiber - The Good News

Harvard researchers did discover an *"inverse association between fiber intake and myocardial infarction."* They concluded that *"fiber,*

---

17. Michels KB, Fuchs CS, Giovannucci E, Colditz GA, Hunter DJ, Stampfer MJ, Willett WC., Obstetrics and Gynecology Epidemiology Center, Department of Obstetrics and Gynecology, Brigham and Women's Hospital, Harvard Medical School, 221 Longwood Avenue, Boston, MA 02115, USA.; *Fiber intake and incidence of colorectal cancer among 76,947 women and 47,279 men.* Cancer Epidemiol Biomarkers Prev. 2005 Apr;14(4):842-9.

18. Brown L, Rosner B, Willett WW, Sacks FM., Department of Nutrition, Harvard School of Public Health, Boston, MA 02115, USA.; *Cholesterol-lowering effects of dietary fiber: a meta-analysis.* Am J Clin Nutr. 1999 Jan;69(1):30-42.

independent of fat intake, is an important dietary component for the prevention of coronary disease."

In simple terms what that means is revolutionary.

Fiber was shown to actually reduce the risk of coronary heart disease by an amazing 40%! Just eating more fiber for the heart healthy benefits alone can potentially save thousands of lives each year.

The news gets better. The Harvard "Nurses Study" also showed that people who had diets higher in cereal fiber had a lower risk of type 2 diabetes. Something as simple as Wheaties or All-Bran and skim milk can potentially give you years of better health.

If that was all fiber could do, it should be enough to convince everyone they need to eat their recommended daily dose. But, researchers also found fiber can help reduce the incidence of diverticular disease AND (here's the big one) it can even help prevent obesity! Here's how.

It takes longer to eat high-fiber foods. Your body has more time to register the food that goes into your stomach and signal your brain you're full. High-fiber meals also tend to be less "energy dense," meaning they have fewer calories compared to a similar volume of low-fiber food. So, if you're trying to lose weight, check out the fiber content of the food you're buying and pick the ones with more fiber per serving.

What is fiber?

It's any part of the plant that can't be digested or absorbed and it's only found in plants. Occasionally you'll hear fiber referred to as roughage or bulk.

Fiber is usually separated into two categories. Insoluble fiber for the ones that don't dissolve in water and Soluble fiber for the ones that do.

Insoluble Fiber helps move things along through your digestive system, providing a good laxative action. It also increases the bulk of your stool helping people who have constipation or irregular stool problems.

You can get insoluble fiber in your diet by eating dried peas and beans, nuts, vegetables, wheat bran and whole-wheat flour.

Soluble Fiber slows digestion and absorption of glucose (sugar), keeping blood sugar levels more even. It can also minimally help reduce blood cholesterol levels.

Sources of soluble fiber can be found in apples, barley, beans, carrots, citrus fruits, lentils, nuts, oats and oatmeal, peas, psyllium and seeds.

Fiber is also available in supplements. Metamucil, Konsyl, Citrucel and FiberCon are four typical brands.

The downside of supplements is they lack many of the vitamins, minerals and other beneficial nutrients that high-fiber foods have. However, they can help if you're unwilling or unable to take in enough fiber through diet alone.

As you add fiber to your diet, do it slowly or during a time of year when the windows can be open all the time, and the neighbors are away on vacation. When you first start eating more you may experience bloating, cramping or gas. Those are all normal reactions and over time your body will adjust. Eventually your neighbors will forgive you, once their property values bounce back to your pre-fiber levels.

Make sure to drink plenty of fluids as well, because liquids help your body digest the fiber better.

Vital Statistic 10 - How much fiber do you need daily?

	Under 50	51 and Over
Men	38 grams	30 Grams
Women	25 grams	21 grams

TAKE ACTION:
Over the next seven days, track your fiber and make sure you're eating enough.

Summary
Fiber

What is Fiber

Any part of the plant that can't be digested or absorbed.

Why do we Need Fiber

Move things along through your digestive system.
Increase the bulk of your stool.
Reduce the risk of coronary heart disease by 40%.
Reduce the risk of type 2 diabetes.
Reduce the incidence of diverticular disease.
Help prevent obesity.

What Foods Have Fiber

Fiber is only found in plants.

Fiber Supplements

Supplements may lack many of the vitamins, minerals and other beneficial nutrients that high-fiber foods have.

Track Your Fiber for a Week

Write down how many grams of fiber you eat every day and see if you're meeting the minimum requirements.

Water

*"For optimum health, everybody should drink eight glasses of water
a day."*

Everybody knows that. It's a given. It's ubiquitous. Some may debate
evolution and climate change, but nobody debates the eight glasses a day
rule. It's just a fact, right?

Not exactly. We began to wonder where the recommendation originally
came from. More importantly, we wanted to know how it applies to people
dieting and working out. We started looking for an answer in 2003.

What we discovered is the "eight glasses of water a day" suggestion isn't
based on research. There's no single study that ever led to that
recommendation. There's not even an agreement about where the idea
originated or who said it first. We would have had an easier time
documenting the family tree of the Sasquatch.

Of course, that doesn't mean drinking reasonable amounts of water is
bad for you. In fact there are dozens of studies that have demonstrated
increased fluid intake is beneficial for combating certain diseases. It's also
a widely documented fact that people who live in hot dry climates and
people who exercise should drink more. It's even been documented that
some diseases thrive when the body is dehydrated.

But what we wanted to know is, how much water should the average
person, and the average athlete, drink every day?

In 2004 the Institute of Medicine of the National Academies (also called
the IOM) released a report called, *Dietary Reference Intakes: Water,
Potassium, Sodium, Chloride, and Sulfate.* The IOM is the organization
responsible for making recommendations on the quantity of nutrients

Americans should be taking in daily. We figured they would give us the answer. Here's what they said.

"The vast majority of healthy people adequately meet their daily hydration needs by letting thirst be their guide. The report did not specify exact requirements for water, but set general recommendations for women at approximately 2.7 liters (91 ounces) of total water — from all beverages and foods — each day, and men an average of approximately 3.7 liters (125 ounces daily) of total water. The panel did not set an upper level for water."

That was it. Unfortunately, it was a number we couldn't use. Unless one were to dehydrate their food to measure water content, there wasn't any way to calculate how much water would be needed. It was a dead end.

Our search was put on hold until March of 2006 when *The American Journal of Clinical Nutrition* released a report called, *A new proposed guidance system for beverage consumption in the United States.* They looked at combinations of all the typical things Americans were drinking and they attempted to calculate how much fluid would be appropriate for each individual.

The study came through with a few recommendations. One was that alcohol consumption should be limited to *"no more than one drink for women and 2 for men (daily). "* They also said sports drinks should be *"consumed sparingly, except by endurance athletes because these beverages provide calories. "*

What did they say about water?

"It is not possible to define a set amount of water for each person because the water needs depend partially on overall diet and the water contained in the foods. "

It was another dead end.

Finally, in March of 2008 Doctors Dan Negoianu and Stanley Goldfarb released a report titled *Just Add Water* where they looked into the eight glasses a day idea along with several others floating around the internet. Here's what the report said.

"There is no clear evidence of benefit from drinking increased amounts of water. Although we wish we could demolish all of the urban myths found on the Internet regarding the benefits of supplemental water ingestion, we concede there is also no clear evidence of lack of benefit. In fact, there is simply a lack of evidence in general."

Dr. Goldfarb said, *"A little mild dehydration for the most part is OK, and a little mild water excess for the most part is OK. It's the extremes that one needs to avoid..."*

That was the answer. **Unless you're drinking a prescribed amount of fluids under doctor's orders, you should let your thirst be your guide. If you're thirsty, drink more. When you're not, stop. It's just that simple.**

Just Add Water also looked at what Dr. Goldfarb and Dr. Negoianu called the "four major myths" surrounding water consumption. This is what they concluded about each myth.

Drinking More Water Helps Speed Toxins Out of the Body - NO
"The kidneys clear toxins. This is what the kidneys do. ...When you take in a lot of water, all you do is put out more urine but not more toxins in the urine."

Drinking More Water Improves Skin Tone - NO
"Although frank dehydration can obviously decrease skin turgor, it is not clear what benefit drinking extra water has for skin...."

Drinking Water Wards off Headaches - MAYBE
"To our knowledge, only one trial has examined headache prevention by increasing water intake. Fifteen patients with migraine headaches were randomly assigned to increased water intake or placebo for 12 [weeks]. The number of hours of headache was quantified over 14-[day] intervals at the beginning and at the end of the trial. Although

the treatment group had 21 fewer hours of headache compared with the control group, this difference did not reach statistical significance (the number of patients was obviously quite small)."

Drinking Water Helps With Weight Loss - MAYBE
"There is surprisingly little evidence regarding this issue. One study of women found water drinking before a meal increased satiety during a meal - but not after it. Caloric intake was not measured. Another study - this time of men - found total caloric intake decreased by increasing the volume of a calorie-containing drink given before the start of a meal. Another study by the same group - of women only - showed increasing the water content of foods themselves decreased caloric intake, but offering water in parallel with food did not. None of these studies makes clear whether drinking a large volume of fluid over the course of a day will decrease the number of ingested calories."

TAKE ACTION:
Stop reading here and get a good nights sleep. Pick the book up again after you're rested.

Summary
Water

How Much Water Should I Drink

Under normal circumstances, unless you're drinking a prescribed amount of fluids under doctor's orders, you should let your thirst be your guide. If you're thirsty, drink more. When you're not, stop. It's just that simple.

In Strenuous Situations Like Exercising and Competitions, How Much Water Should I Drink

If you're competing or training for some athletic event, ask your doctor or health care provider how much water you'll need and follow their instructions. In strenuous situations thirst may NOT be an appropriate guide. Follow the advice of medical professionals.

Salt (Sodium)

Salt is a dietary mineral that's essential to all animal life on earth. We use it to regulate the fluid balance in our bodies. It also helps preserve food and adds flavoring to the majority of pre-packaged items found in grocery stores.

Like everything else, moderation is the key. Unfortunately, right now people around the world are eating far too much and it's killing us. In fact, an analysis published in *The Lancet Chronic Diseases Series* in 2007 concluded that if global salt intake could be cut by just 15%, 8.5 million deaths would be prevented by 2015. That means more than a million people are dying every year from consuming too much salt!

Eating too much salt has been linked to high blood pressure, increased risk of heart attack, stroke and impaired blood vessel function. It's the silent killer few are willing to talk about.

We want to make it clear that we're not saying everybody should stop eating salt. Even if that were possible, it wouldn't be healthy. We're saying we need to cut down to levels that *are* healthy.

Pop Quiz! How much salt does the United States Department of Agriculture (USDA) suggest a healthy adult consume daily?

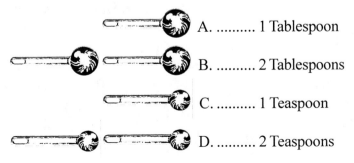

A. .... 1 Tablespoon

B. .... 2 Tablespoons

C. .... 1 Teaspoon

D. .... 2 Teaspoons

ANSWER: (c) 1 teaspoon or about 2,300 milligrams. That's the TOTAL amount you should take in from everything you eat and drink. However, the average American consumes more than 3,400 milligrams of sodium daily. That's nearly a third more than we should.

The exact amount each person requires can vary greatly. People who are active or sweat a lot generally need more while inactive people need less. Fortunately, figuring out approximately how much you need is relatively simple. As always you can get this information on our website at www.DietisDead.com.

11 - How much salt should I eat?

If you work out or sweat a lot, take the total amount of calories you should be eating and multiply that number by 125%.

If you don't exercise, simply take the total calories and multiply it by 100% (so the milligrams of sodium would equal the number of calories per day).

See your doctor or health care provider before you take in more than 2,400 miligrams of sodium daily, no matter what the previous two calculations told you.

The answer is the maximum milligrams of sodium you should take in daily.

Once you have an idea how much salt you need, it's important to track it so you know if you're getting too much.

The first step is to learn where salt is hiding. This is where it gets a little tricky. Salt is added to everything from breakfast cereals to canned vegetables. Packaged meals and soups often have more than half the United States Recommended Daily Allowance (USRDA) in a single serving. Salt is routinely added to so many different foods that when companies want to stand out they make a point of putting "No Salt Added" on the label.

There are essentially three forms of salt used for human consumption.

Unrefined salt, such as sea salts, come in different colors and are distinguished by their grain, the minerals they're mixed with and the methods used to harvest them.

Refined salt, more commonly called **table salt** is often mined or brought to the surface through injected water. If refined salt has any extraneous minerals attached, they're removed.

Iodized salt is simply refined salt mixed with a minimum amount of potassium iodide, sodium iodide or iodate. The iodized salt is then able to prevent and remedy iodine deficiency, which is the leading preventable cause of mental retardation.

Don't bother switching from one type of salt to another for health reasons. All salt, no matter what form it comes in, has about the same sodium content when compared ounce for ounce.

Here are some ways to cut back on your salt intake.

Take the salt shaker off the table. Put it away in a cabinet and stop adding it to food once it's prepared. You might be surprised how many things taste fine, just the way they are.

Buy vegetables that are fresh, frozen or canned without added salt. Something as simple as a can of tomatoes can have over 200 milligrams of sodium lurking in a single serving. The "No Salt Added" tomatoes have around 50 milligrams per serving.

Substitute lemon juice, herbs and spices whenever salt is called for in a recipe. When you use less salt in a dish it allows the rich flavors of all the other ingredients to come out.

Skip the breaded, marinated and processed meats for the unprocessed ones. You'll spend less money and be able to spice foods how you want.

Be sure to check the label, even on items you wouldn't normally suspect of having sodium, to make sure you have an accurate count. Then check the sodium level against the total calories. If the sodium is more than 125% the total number of calories, choose another brand or type of food.

TAKE ACTION:
Switch to products with "No Salt Added"
and take the salt shaker off your table.

Summary
Salt

How Much Salt Daily is Acceptable

According to the USDA a healthy adult should consume no more than 1 teaspoon of salt daily, about 2,300 miligrams. That's total salt in everything you eat and drink.

How to Track Salt

If you work out or sweat a lot, take the total amount of calories you should be eating and multiply that number by 125%.

If you don't exercise, simply take the total calories and multiply it by 100% (so the milligrams of sodium would equal the number of calories per day).

Don't go over 2,400 milligrams of sodium daily without a doctor's approval, no matter what the previous two calculations told you.

Don't Bother Switching

The sodium levels in all three common salt forms is essentially the same. Switching between refined, unrefined or idodized won't make a difference.

•

Fruit

Fruit has been getting a bad rap for quite a while now. It's the food group that seems to cause the most dietary confusion, and the one that people we train most often bring up when they ask about what to cut back on. The problem isn't the fruit; it's what people are being told about fruit that's the problem.

The recent batch of misinformation started with the United States government in 1992. That's when the United States Department of Agriculture (USDA) released the food pyramid. On that chart it said Americans should get "2-4 servings of fruit per day." The problem was the chart didn't have a definition of exactly how much fruit was in a serving. It also didn't distinguish between how many servings for men and how many for women.

Fruit was vilified throughout the 1990s by the low-carb craze. Instead of eating healthy servings in moderation, people stopped eating it altogether and substituted higher fat and lower fiber options. Of course that didn't help, and Americans just kept getting fatter.

In 2005 two significant things happened to start rehabilitating the image of fruit. First the low-carb craze finally started to subside. Only 53% of the people who started an Atkins low-carb program stayed on the diet for a year. Of the people who stayed on the diet, total weight loss over a year was less than five pounds.[19]

---

19. Dansinger ML, Gleason JA, Griffith JL, Selker HP, Schaefer EJ., Division of Endocrinology, Diabetes, and Metabolism, Atherosclerosis Research Laboratory, Tufts-New England Medical Center, Boston, Mass 02111, USA.; *Comparison of the Atkins, Ornish, Weight Watchers, and Zone diets for weight loss and heart disease risk reduction: a randomized trial.* Journal of the American Medical Association. 2005 Jan 5;293(1):43-53.

The second thing that happened was the revised USDA food pyramid. In the new one the generic "2-4 servings of fruit per day" was replaced with specific recommendations for men, women and children. In a nutshell, women should aim for 1.5 cups of fruit a day, while men should shoot for 2 cups. If you're exercising and burning more calories, it's suggested that those numbers go up even higher.

Now, before you go trying to overcompensate for all your missed fruit opportunities, keep in mind I'm talking about the whole fruit, NOT fruit juice. That's where even the updated food pyramid falls short. It says "any fruit or 100% fruit juice counts as part of the fruit group. Fruits may be fresh, canned, frozen, or dried, and may be whole, cut-up, or pureed."

If you want truly healthy servings of fruit, you should discount that bit of advice because there are three major problems with it.

Fruit is not the problem, fruit juice is.

First, fruit juice tends to be much more "calorie dense" than whole fruit. One whole large orange has about 86 calories and 4.5 grams of fiber. A small 12 oz. glass of orange juice has twice the calories (about 167), and less than 1 gram of fiber. Drinking fruit instead of eating it typically doubles or triples the calories while eliminating much of the healthy fiber.

Second, canned fruit is often packed in "syrup" to make it taste better. Syrup is a marketing word for added sugar. There's already plenty of sugar (as fructose) in fruit without more being poured on top. Canned fruit can be healthy, just be sure to buy the ones with nothing added.

Finally, be very careful before eating dried fruit. A medium sized banana has 107 calories, 14 grams of sugar, and when cut up, fills about a cup. But, if you were to eat a cup of dried banana chips, that has a whopping 436 calories and more than half your daily allowance of sugar, 30 grams.

To make it even worse many companies add salt or mix fattening foods like chocolate, coconut or salted nuts in with bags of dried fruit. If you're in a situation where dried fruit is the only convenient source of fruit, eat it sparingly; avoid mixing it with unhealthy extras and pay close attention to the total calories and serving size.

TAKE ACTION:
The next time you go to the grocery store, pickup seven servings (at least 1.5 cups per serving) of whole fruit for the week.

Summary
Fruit

Fruit is Good for You

Eat whole fruit.

Avoid fruit juices, candy coated fruits, dried fruit or anything packed in syrup.

Women should eat about 1.5 cups of whole fruit a day.

Men should eat about 2 cups of whole fruit a day.

Meal Timing

"When should I stop eating at night?" It's a question we hear over and over from people trying to lose weight. There is this mythical belief that calories consumed late at night are somehow worse than those eaten at any other time during the day, as if we were distant relatives of Gremlins, and shouldn't be fed after midnight.

Diet programs like Atkins, South Beach and Weight Watchers encourage the late night ban and all warn against bedtime dining. The problem is, that idea appears to be seriously flawed. After all, isn't a calorie the same no matter when it's eaten? If you're on a diet that limits you to 2,000 calories, what's the difference if you eat it all in one sitting or in little bits throughout the day?

The most popular theory behind the ban is based on metabolism. Your metabolic rate decreases during sleep, so consuming a lot of calories before bedtime can cause the calories to burn more slowly. Your body would supposedly store more fat and weight gain would be the result.

Well that's true...sort of. The act of digesting food does burn calories. If you eat several small meals throughout the day, your inner furnace does work more consistently and you do burn slightly more calories. But it's a little more involved than that.

More important than the storage of fat is the loss of muscle. Throughout the day your body needs energy. As a general rule, the food in your stomach, the last meal you ate, is where your body's energy comes from.

A typical meal takes two to four hours to digest. If it's been longer than four hours, you still need energy but there's no food left in your stomach to draw from. Now your body has two choices; it can draw energy from muscle or fat. Guess which one it uses up first?

Muscle, and here's why. A pound of muscle burns about three times as many calories per day as a pound of fat. If you were living before modern conveniences, the last thing you would want is a bunch of muscle, burning up calories and making you hungry. Remember, until the last 100 years or so food was always in limited supply.

Your body tries to get rid of any muscle by burning it up for energy first. You shed muscle at every opportunity and hang onto the fat. In the past, having a nice layer of fat was important to keep you warm and help you avoid starving to death during the winter. Today, all that fat simply leads to disease and an early death.

If you're waiting until late at night to eat the majority of your calories, your body has been eating up muscle all day to keep you going.

Skipping meals burns muscle, not fat.

Even more critical than dinner is when you eat breakfast. When you first wake up your body generally hasn't had food in several hours, so your metabolism has slowed down to conserve energy. Eating breakfast boosts your metabolism and helps you burn up to ten percent more calories doing your morning activities. The total number of extra calories you burn isn't significant. But, the fact your body STOPS burning muscle IS a big deal.

Metabolism isn't the only reason you should eat every two to four hours, food choice is another. If you skip a meal, you're more likely to eat high-calorie and high-fat foods when you get hungry. Small frequent meals help you avoid that "starving" feeling and subsequent food binges.

There is one more critical time you need to make sure to eat, and that's after your workout. Glycogen synthesis (your muscle's ability to repair itself) is higher immediately after a workout than if you wait as long as two hours later. It doesn't even seem to make much difference what carbs you eat, just as long as you eat something.[20] The sooner you eat or drink after exercise, the better your recovery rate.

Eating most of your food late at night won't significantly change your weight. But, if you consume most of your calories all in one meal your body will lose more muscle and hang onto more fat. The best advice is simple. Eat early, eat often and practice moderation at every meal. It works.

---

20. Kreider RB, Earnest CP, Lundberg J, Rasmussen C, Greenwood M, Cowan P, Almada AL., Exercise & Sport Nutrition Lab, Center for Exercise, Nutrition and Preventive Health, Baylor University, Waco, TX, USA; *Effects of ingesting protein with various forms of carbohydrate following resistance-exercise on substrate availability and markers of anabolism, catabolism, and immunity.* Journal of the International Society of Sports Nutrition. 2007 Nov 12;4:18.

TAKE ACTION:
Block out space on your schedule to eat at least three meals and two snacks a day. Space them two to four hours apart.

Summary
Meal Timing

Make Eating Important

Schedule a breakfast, lunch and dinner every day, no matter what.

Eat something that's higher in carbs and protein within 30 minutes of getting up and after working out.

Bring along food for at least two healthy snacks a day.

Don't eat food the last hour before you go to bed. It's not because of weight gain, but rather because the act of digesting food may keep you awake.

Emotional Eating

If you've ever eaten because you were depressed, worried or stressed out, you're not alone. It's called "emotional eating" and we do it because, at least temporarily, eating food that's not very good for us can make us feel better.

Recognizing the link between emotion and eating isn't new. During World War I, people noticed that soldiers' widows frequently put on weight. They discovered that widows were using food as a way to cope with the grief and loss. There's even a word for it in German, "kummerspeck." Literally translated it means "grief bacon."

While emotional eating was known, it wasn't studied much because food wasn't as readily available as it is today. Obesity was a problem generally confined to rich people.

As food became more available, and with the huge proliferation of fast and convenience foods, eating disorders started appearing in middle and lower income groups. The number of people who engaged in physical work steadily dropped as labor saving devices were introduced. The combination of all these factors led to increasingly higher levels of obesity.

Scientists started looking into the problem to find out the underlying mechanisms. One of the causes they discovered were brain chemicals called neurotransmitters. Specifically, dopamine, norepinephrine and serotonin.

It seems that when serotonin levels in the brain are higher, the person is more calm. Serotonin has an anxiety reducing effect and in some people it promotes drowsiness. Keeping serotonin levels stable in the brain is associated with a positive mood state.

That's where your diet comes in. Foods that are high in carbohydrates increase the levels of serotonin. Breads, pasta, cereals and candy are all capable of producing a temporary increase in the serotonin levels…and calming us down.

Some emotional eating is rooted in the technology explosion that started in the late 1980s and continues today. We've become a nation of people who are "always on." Before the 1980s if people wanted to get in touch with you, they could call. If you were privileged enough to have an answering machine they could leave a message. In the late 1980s and early 1990s cell phones and answering devices became ubiquitous.

Today we're expected to be available to everybody at a moment's notice. Add the rise of email, instant or text messaging and hardly a minute goes by when someone can't get in touch with you somehow. For some, just the anticipation can be enough of a stressor to trigger emotional eating.

All that access has a price. Being available all the time has increased our levels of anxiety, leading to more emotional eating. As the weight goes on, more eating takes place to handle the negative feelings and the weight spirals up.

To avoid stuffing yourself with food because of the way you feel, make yourself less available.

Turn off your cell phone when you need to concentrate or want some uninterrupted time. If you work on a computer, turn off the notification system that pops up every time you get a new email. Designate a couple times during the day when you answer your phone calls and respond to emails. You'll get more done when you're not constantly interrupted and your levels of anxiety will drop, without resorting to emotional eating.

You should also take an honest look at your eating habits. If you're using food on a daily basis to cope with life, you may need the help of a professional to deal with the disorder. Make an appointment with a therapist or look for a local chapter of overeaters anonymous.

Ways to cope with overeating.

Start writing down things that trigger your eating. When you want to grab some comfort food, ask yourself why. Are you bored? Do something to engage your mind. Read a book, play a game or explore a hobby. Are you feeling overlooked? Do something to pamper yourself. Give yourself a facial. Sit in a hot tub, swim in a pool or just take a relaxing bath.

Don't try to eliminate unhealthy foods overnight, look for substitutions. If you like ice cream, buy the lower fat and lower calorie single serving options. If chocolate is your thing, look for fat and sugar free puddings.

Practice portion control. Instead of eating the entire meal in one setting, cut the serving in half. Eat half now and wait 30 minutes. Then, if you're still hungry, you can eat more.

Consider that some over-eating may be the result of pills. Inventory your prescriptions, over the counter medications and supplements. Some of them, such as ones used to treat depression or bipolar disorder, are appetite stimulants. If they are, talk with your doctor or pharmacist about alternatives that don't cause cravings.

Before you indulge, exercise. If you want to eat a 200 calorie snack bar, exercise those 200 calories off before you take the first bite. The exercise helps release endorphins which make you feel better, and once you finish your exercise, the cravings may have passed.

Keep a food journal. Write down everything you eat and drink. You don't have to use it to calculate every little thing in the food, it's just to make you more aware of what you eat. Sometimes just the thought of writing down that cheat food will give you the willpower to avoid it.

Finally, if you really are hungry and it's not just emotions, decide what balanced meal you're going to eat and enjoy.

TAKE ACTION:
Keep a food log to track when and why
you're eating. Look for emotional triggers.

Summary
Emotional Eating

Reduce Interruptions

Make yourself less available. Schedule times when you don't answer the phone, email or text messages. You'll do more in less time.

Keep a Food Log

Write down things that trigger your eating.

Log everything you eat and drink to see where all the calories are coming from.

Substitute healthier foods for the full calorie varieties.

Food Labels in a Hurry

Grocery shopping is one of those things that always used to take me much longer than I liked. Even when I had a list of exactly what I needed, and knew where it was located in the store, inevitably I ended up comparing different brands, measuring one product against the other until I found the one with the best nutritional profile.

Once I stood in the aisle and spent ten minutes reading every single peanut butter label to find out the one that was lowest in fat, sugar and sodium.

There had to be a better way. I figured I should be able to look at a nutrition label and decide in eight seconds or less if something was good for me or not. So, I designed what I call "food label shorthand" to figure things out in an instant. This is how you do it.

(At the end of this chapter is a quick reference guide you can use at the supermarket. As you read each section, look at the quick reference guide to see where it's located.)

<u>Start with the serving size and calories.</u> Even when it looks like a single serving package, read how many servings are supposed to come out. I picked up a snack mix the other day that looked like enough for two people. But, the serving size on the label said it was for seven and it had 120 calories per serving! With two of us eating half the small bag each, that would have been a gut bomb of 420 calories per person.

Soda and sports drinks are notorious for this trick. Many brands are sold in convenient 16 oz. plastic bottles that show the nutritional information for a single serving, but the container actually holds two. If the serving size is too small to be realistic, put it back on the shelf.

Next, move down to the part of the label that says "calories from fat." It's directly under the heading "calories." If the calories from fat number is higher than 30% of the calories, it's too high in fat according to the United States Department of Agriculture (USDA).

An easy way to get a rough idea is to divide the total calories by three. The number you come up with should be HIGHER than the calories from fat.

Avoid anything that has Trans Fat in it. The only acceptable number here is zero. Because food companies can claim zero if there's less than five grams per serving, you also need to check the ingredient list when you're looking at crackers, cakes, cookies, muffins or other baked goods. Foods with the words or phrases, "Partially Hydrogenated Oils, Shortening, Interesterified or Stearate-Rich" all contain unhealthy trans fats.

Sodium is the next candidate. Compare the milligrams of sodium to the calories. If both numbers are the same, or if the sodium is lower, the food has a reasonable to low amount of sodium in it. When the sodium number is more than 25% higher than the calories, it probably has too much salt to be healthy and you should consider skipping it unless it's a very small serving.

Check out the fiber now. Three grams or more per serving is a good start. If there's more fiber in a food, it slows down the digestion for a sustained release of energy. When choosing between two foods, if all else is equal, buy the one that has more fiber.

At this point, I've sorted out much of the junk food. I've also been able to quickly compare several options and pick the healthier one. There are only three more things to consider.

Sugar is tricky. There are no requirements to show how much sugar is acceptable in the average diet. The World Health Organization (WHO) estimates that someone eating 2,000 calories a day should keep it between 45g and 55g per day.

To make sure you're not taking in too much sugar, memorize this formula: Keep sugar to 1 gram per 40 calories. If you eat something with more sugar, you'll need to compensate later by taking in less during other meals.

That takes me to protein. If everything else is equal, choose the brand that's higher in protein. Don't worry about getting too much. That's pretty rare in the modern American diet.

Finally, check out the ingredients list. When you're looking at two different foods that are virtually identical nutritionally, pick the one with fewer ingredients. In commercial products that usually means it has the least amount of artificial preservatives and flavorings.

With a little practice, you should be able to scan a label in under eight seconds and decide if it's something that might be good for you, or something that would be better left on the supermarket shelf.

 TAKE ACTION: Bring the Quick Reference Guide (pages 132-133) along with you next time you go shopping.

Food Labels in a Hurry - *Quick Reference*

Is serving size realistic?

Are calories from fat less
than 30% of total calories?
(Calories ÷ 3. The answer should
be HIGHER than calories from fat.)

Avoid Partially Hydrogenated Oils,
Shortening, Interesterified or
Stearate-Rich.

Is sodium number lower
than 125% of calories number?

Is fiber 3g or higher per serving?

Is sugar 1g per 40 calories or less?

Does it have any protein?

Ingredients

When you're looking at two foods that are nearly the same nutritionally, pick the one with fewer ingredients. In commercial products that usually means it has the least amount of artificial preservatives and flavorings.

Nutrition Facts

Serving Size: 1/2 cup dry (40g)
Servings Per Container 30

Amount Per Serving

Calories	150
Calories from Fat	25

% Daily Value*

Total Fat 3g	5%
Saturated Fat 0.5	2%
Trans Fat	0%
Cholesterol 0mg	0%
Sodium 0mg	0%
Total Carb 27g	9%
Dietary Fiber 4g	15%
Sugars 1g	
Protein 5g	

	Calories:	2,000	2,500
Total Fat	Less than	65g	80g
Sat Fat	Less than	20g	25g
Cholesterol	Less than	300mg	300mg
Sodium	Less than	2,400mg	2,400mg
Total Carbohydrate		300g	375g
Dietary Fiber		25g	30g

Summary
Food Labels in a Hurry

Take Time to Compare

When you first start comparing food labels it's going to
take a little time. Pick two things you buy regularly to
compare each shopping trip.

Once you find a healthier option you enjoy, make that
your regular choice. Over time a healthy shopping trip
won't take any longer than your unhealthy ones.

Bring the Nutrition Facts Guide Every Time

There are eight primary things to compare on every nutrition label. You don't have to memorize all the information,
just bring the handy chart with you every time. Whenever
you're tempted to try a new packaged food, check it out
before you buy to make sure you're not sabotaging your
diet.

Make a Menu

The success or failure of any diet is based on one simple thing: how many calories you eat each day. Eat more than you burn and you gain weight. Eat less than you burn and you'll lose weight.

The first half of this book is designed to teach you about the individual components in food. What they are, why they're important and how to identify them in the foods you eat. Now it's time to figure out exactly what to eat. This is where many diet books fail.

A traditional diet book uses this section to give you the "hook." That's their big idea to help you dramatically lose all the weight, and it's presented as a shortcut. Those books imply that if you follow that one simple rule for the rest of your life, a world of health and fitness will be laid at your feet.

Over the years diet books have said you should eliminate carbs, drop the fat, increase the protein or concentrate on a single food type. Fitness companies have told you to exercise more, juice companies have told you to drink more and drug companies have told you that taking a pill is the answer. Oh, and here's a coupon to get you started.

Each one of those ideas work, as long as you're willing to follow someone else's plan. That's also their biggest downfall. People don't like change. On page 16 (the chapter about Taking Action) we told you that not only are humans resistant to change, but we become more set in our ways the older we get.

Dramatic changes generally happen one of two ways. Either you experience a traumatic event or you get there through small steps. As you've finished each chapter, you've taken small steps to learn what's in the food you're eating and how to identify healthier alternatives.

Then we showed you how to put all those tips together and read the nutritional labels quickly. Now you're going to use that knowledge to design a diet plan that's just for you.

You're going to make a menu.

It's time to take 30 minutes and plan out everything you're going to eat for the next seven days. Your menu should revolve around the types of foods you enjoy eating. Meat eaters, vegetarians and vegans can each stick with their beliefs. By teaching you what to look for, it's our goal to help you make healthier and more balanced choices within your food preferences.

Here are three ways to make a menu.

1. Menu plan we included.

Choose from one of our pre-made options. At the end of this chapter we've put together one set of meal plans for meat eaters and another for vegetarians. Then they're divided into week long options with daily limits of approximately 1,200 and 1,500 calories. Choose which one is most appropriate, based on your daily calorie requirements.

2. Fill out our Food and Drink Log Sheet on page 50.

Use our Food and Drink Log Sheet to plan what you're GOING to eat. Each day you choose the foods that'll work best for your taste and lifestyle. Write down their calories, fat, protein and carbs to make a balanced day. You can download and print additional copies of the Food and Drink Log Sheet on our website, www.DietisDead.com and click on "Food Logs."

3. See our website.

Visit our website www.DietisDead.com under the "Food Logs" button where we've put links to several companies that will create menus based on your particular caloric needs, preferences and even medical restrictions.

Menu Design Tips

Involve all family members in menu planning. Give each person the chance to talk about their food likes and dislikes, favorite recipes, and what they'd like to see on the family menu. Give everybody a task such as helping out with shopping for food, unpacking groceries, setting the table, or cooking.

Start with the main attraction. Decide on the main course for each meal over the coming week. Think about food your family enjoys, your budget, the time you have to prepare the food, and nutrition.

Mix it up. Try to introduce one new main course each week, so that your family gets to experience new tastes. Adding new main courses also makes it more likely that your family members will get all the nutrients they need.

Use leftovers. Look for chances to use the leftovers from one meal for another meal later in the week.

Don't make any dramatic reductions in calories. It seems like a good idea at first. Eating too much causes weight gain, so if you cut back on your calories you should lose weight fast. Unfortunately, your body doesn't know you're going on a diet.

If there's a large drop in calories, your body goes into starvation mode and hangs onto all the fat it can. You start burning muscle for energy and your metabolism slows down to conserve body mass. After a few weeks the weight loss stops and your body adjusts to the lower food intake. Even worse, you've now lost some metabolism boosting muscle and hung onto unhealthy fat.

A better plan is to only drop calories down 10-20% from your current level. It'll create a caloric deficit without triggering a plunge in your metabolism. Once a week enjoy a "cheat meal" where you eat a little more. The increase short-circuits your body's adaptation response so your metabolic rate doesn't start moving down.

<u>Remember to keep your menu realistic.</u> If you've never cooked before, don't expect you'll whip up a gourmet meal every night for dinner. Plan simple or frozen meals for when you're in a hurry and more elaborate or cook ahead meals when you've got time. Don't forget to include snacks for quick pick-me-ups.

<u>Look for recipes you can cook in advance and freeze.</u> It saves a tremendous amount of time and allows you to re-heat something healthy in minutes. To spend even less time in the kitchen, choose recipes that can be cooked together in one pot. Casseroles, stir-fry dishes or crock pot meals can all save cooking and clean up time.

At the top of the sheet, write down how many calories you're allowed to have each day. Make a separate sheet for each day of the week. Start making those menus!

TAKE ACTION:
Before you go shopping again, make a menu or choose a menu that matches your nutritional requirements and preferences.

Summary
Make a Menu

Making a Menu is the Secret

If you continue buying, ordering and preparing the same food you've always had, you'll continue getting the same results. You must look at your schedule, one week at a time and design a healthy menu you can stick to.

If you don't have the time to prepare your own food, you need to include prepared meals and healthy restaurant options on your menu.

Don't Plan for Rapid Weight Loss

Don't dramatically reduce your calories unless instructed by a doctor or health care professional. Slow and steady is the healthiest and most sustainable way to lose weight. Losing one to two pounds a week is reasonable.

Daily Menus

In a typical diet book, the meal plans they list show generic foods that taste bland or name brand items that may or may not be available in your supermarket. The authors also tend to lump everyone into a group and suggest the entire world should eat the exact same thing.

This is different. The following pages contain four different six-day menus. They're divided into two for meat eaters and two for vegetarians; based on 1,200 and 1,500 calorie a day requirements. We chose a very general nutritional breakdown of 25% protein, 25% fat and the remainder (50%) carbohydrates.

There is a wide variety of foods presented in the following pages because over the course of each 6-day plan we tried not to duplicate the same meal. That will give you the widest variety of choices when you're making YOUR menu.

These plans may not be the right ones for you!

Our goal throughout this book has been to help you figure out what YOU need to eat. How many calories you should take in. What percentage of your calories should be fat, protein and carbs.

If you're trying to gain weight, these menus may not have enough calories. If you have a specific medical condition requiring diet modifications, you won't find those allowances here. If you have food allergies, live someplace without a kitchen or are in a country where the foods we talk about aren't available, these menus may not work.

Rather than a mandate of what you must eat, think of these menus as a source of inspiration. Use them for ideas when you design YOUR daily menu based on YOUR SPECIFIC requirements.

There's also another surprise. Every food item with a W beside it can be found online at www.WeCookFit.com. We won't waste space in this book filling it with recipes when we can post hundreds of them online FREE for you to choose the ones you want.

For quick access to the recipes from menus as they appear in this book, go to wwwDietisDead.com and click on "Daily Menus." You'll see each day and a link to the recipes listed. Any recipe that has the words "Freezer Friendly" underneath it can be prepared in advance and frozen, to be reheated later when you want to eat.

Your goal is to design a menu based on YOUR requirements and not what WE think you should be eating.

One more thing. The following menus have plenty of flaws. Some are too high in carbs, some don't have enough fat and others are low in fiber. While each individual day may not be perfect, the goal is to eat a broad variety of healthier food over the course of a week. These are ideas to help you think of ways to do that.

1,200 Calorie - All Foods
25% Protein, 25% Fat, 50% Carbohydrates
6 Day Plan (Day 1)

Breakfast

	Cal	Fat	Pro	Carb
W Scrambled Egg Sandwich	292	2.4	28	37

Mid Morning Snack

	Cal	Fat	Pro	Carb
8 Cauliflower Flowerets	26	.1	2.1	5.5
8 Medium Baby Carrots	28	.1	.5	6.6
2 Tablespoons Reduced Fat Ranch	66	5.2	.3	4.9

Lunch

	Cal	Fat	Pro	Carb
W Corn Chowder with Chicken	158	2.6	15	21

Afternoon Snack

	Cal	Fat	Pro	Carb
1 Medium Apple	95	.3	.5	25.1
2 Tablespoons Peanut Butter	188	16.1	8	6.3

Dinner

	Cal	Fat	Pro	Carb
W 1 Salsa Chicken - Crock Pot	419	6.1	42.5	45

	Cal	Fat	Pro	Carb
Totals	**1272**	**32.9**	**96.8**	**151.4**
GOAL	**1200**	**33.3**	**75**	**150**

1,200 Calorie - All Foods
25% Protein, 25% Fat, 50% Carbohydrates
6 Day Plan (Day 2)

Breakfast

	Cal	Fat	Pro	Carb
W 2 Slices of Crispy French Toast	380	9.4	21	65

Mid Morning Snack

| W 1 Apple Juice Protein Shake .... | 143 | 1 | 17 | 16 |

Lunch

| W Tomato & Tofu Soup .... | 165 | 2.7 | 9 | 26 |

Afternoon Snack

| W Peach Protein Bar............................... | 110 | 2.0 | 6.5 | 16.5 |

Dinner

| W Taco Salad .... | 394 | 10 | 30 | 46 |

| **Totals** .... | **1192** | **25** | **83.5** | **169.5** |
| **GOAL** .... | **1200** | **33.3** | **75** | **150** |

1,200 Calorie - All Foods
25% Protein, 25% Fat, 50% Carbohydrates
6 Day Plan (Day 3)

Breakfast

	Cal	Fat	Pro	Carb
W Roasted Asparagus & Eggs	132	3.6	15	13

Mid Morning Snack

1 Medium Banana	105	.4	1.3	27
6 Raw Almonds	42	3.6	1.5	1.4

Lunch

W Hawaiian Bagel	297	6	16	46

Afternoon Snack

W Lemon Plum Cheesecake Protein Shake				
....	196	1	18	29

Dinner

W Chicken Cacciatore	463	13	50	32

Totals	**1235**	**27.6**	**101.8**	**148.4**
GOAL	**1200**	**33.3**	**75**	**150**

1,200 Calorie - All Foods
25% Protein, 25% Fat, 50% Carbohydrates
6 Day Plan (Day 4)

Breakfast

	Cal	Fat	Pro	Carb
W Sausage, Red Pepper & Grits Casserole	277	5	25	30

Mid Morning Snack

	Cal	Fat	Pro	Carb
1 Cup Chopped Broccoli Raw	31	.3	2.6	6
2 Tablespoons Fat Free Thousand Island ..	42	.5	.2	9.4

Lunch

	Cal	Fat	Pro	Carb
W Grilled Turkey and Swiss Sandwich	339	9.6	26	38

Afternoon Snack

	Cal	Fat	Pro	Carb
W Pear Protein Bar	137	4	7.5	19

Dinner

	Cal	Fat	Pro	Carb
W Stuffed Green Bell Peppers	352	8	36	36

	Cal	Fat	Pro	Carb
Totals	**1178**	**27.4**	**97.2**	**138.4**
GOAL	**1200**	**33.3**	**75**	**150**

1,200 Calorie - All Foods
25% Protein, 25% Fat, 50% Carbohydrates
6 Day Plan (Day 5)

Breakfast

	Cal	Fat	Pro	Carb
W 3 Chocolate Chip Protein Pancakes ...	372	9.4	31	42

Mid Morning Snack

W 1 Whole Wheat Energy Bar	232	6.3	11.4	37

Lunch

W Chilled English Pea and Mint Soup	205	1	14	36

Afternoon Snack

10 Medium Baby Carrots	35	.1	.6	8.2

Dinner

W Glazed Pork Tenderloin	355	6	45	30

	Cal	Fat	Pro	Carb
Totals	**1199**	**22.8**	**102**	**153.2**
GOAL	**1200**	**33.3**	**75**	**150**

1,200 Calorie - All Foods
25% Protein, 25% Fat, 50% Carbohydrates
6 Day Plan (Day 6)

Breakfast

	Cal	Fat	Pro	Carb
W Tuna and Eggs Benedict 336	3.3	42	31

Mid Morning Snack

	Cal	Fat	Pro	Carb
1 Cup Fiber One Honey Cluster Cereal ... 160	1.5	5	42
1 cup 1% Lowfat Milk 105	2.4	8.5	12.2

Lunch

	Cal	Fat	Pro	Carb
W Peanut Butter and Chocolate Banana Sandwich 230	7	15	27

Afternoon Snack

	Cal	Fat	Pro	Carb
W Sweet and Sour Chicken Salad 194	5	19	18

Dinner

	Cal	Fat	Pro	Carb
W Mustard Wine Chicken (One-Dish) 217	7.7	27	.5

	Cal	Fat	Pro	Carb
Totals	**1242**	**26.9**	**116.5**	**130.7**
GOAL	**1200**	**33.3**	**75**	**150**

1,500 Calorie - All Foods
25% Protein, 25% Fat, 50% Carbohydrates
6 Day Plan (Day 1)

Breakfast

	Cal	Fat	Pro	Carb
W Tomato-Zucchini Frittata	151	5	16.3	11
1/4 of a Medium Cantaloupe Melon	69	.4	1.7	17.9

Mid Morning Snack

4 Medium Stalks Celery	22	.3	1.1	5.5
2 Tablespoons Peanut Butter....................	188	16.1	8	6.3

Lunch

W 1 Bacon Benedictine Sandwich	304	8.1	19	37

Afternoon Snack

W 1 Blueberry Protein Shake	246	1.3	16	44

Dinner

W 1 Beef and Soba Noodle Salad	535	14	42	63

Totals	**1516**	**45.2**	**104.1**	**184.6**
GOAL	**1500**	**41.7**	**93.7**	**187.5**

1,500 Calorie - All Foods
25% Protein, 25% Fat, 50% Carbohydrates
6 Day Plan (Day 2)

Breakfast

	Cal	Fat	Pro	Carb
W 2 Pecan Yam Protein Pancakes	331	7.9	21.1	43.6

Mid Morning Snack

W 1 Banana Cream Protein Bar	146	2.3	8.5	22
12 Walnut Halves	164	16.3	3.8	3.4

Lunch

W 1 Sloppy Joe (With Optional Salt)	335	7.8	32	36

Afternoon Snack

20 Seedless Grapes	68	.2	.7	17.7
20 Sugar Pea Pods	29	.1	1.9	5.1

Dinner

W 1 Cranberry Turkey Nut Salad	341	9	46	16
1 Slice 100% Whole Wheat Bread	100	1.5	5	20

Totals	**1512**	**45.1**	**119**	**163.9**
GOAL	**1500**	**41.7**	**93.7**	**187.5**

1,500 Calorie - All Foods
25% Protein, 25% Fat, 50% Carbohydrates
6 Day Plan (Day 3)

Breakfast

	Cal	Fat	Pro	Carb
W 1 Peanut Butter & Jelly Stuffed French Toast 386	386	11	24	57
1/4 Cup Cary's Sugar Free Syrup 30	30	0	0	12

Mid Morning Snack

49 Kernels (1 oz.) Raw Pistachios 158	158	12.6	5.8	7.9

Lunch

W 1 Monte Cristo Sandwich 444	444	13	40	49

Afternoon Snack

W 1 Coconut Strawberry Protein Shake . 183	183	3.5	18	20

Dinner

W 1 Serving Baked Beans 210	210	.5	10	44
6 Asparagus Spears, Steamed 24	24	.1	2.6	4.7

Totals 1435	1435	40.7	100.5	194.6
GOAL 1500	1500	41.7	93.7	187.5

1,500 Calorie - All Foods
25% Protein, 25% Fat, 50% Carbohydrates
6 Day Plan (Day 4)

Breakfast

	Cal	Fat	Pro	Carb
W 1 Cinnamon Fruit Filled Crepe	140	1	10	23
1 Cup 1% Milk	105	2.4	8.5	12.2

Mid Morning Snack

W 1 Mini-Loaf Blueberry Protein Bread .	247	2.6	18	37

Lunch

W Vegetable Lentil Soup	259	2.4	15	43

Afternoon Snack

1 Serving (1 oz.) Triscuit Baked Whole Wheat Crackers	120	4.5	3	19
2 Slices (1 oz. each) Low-fat Cheddar	97	3.9	13.6	1.1

Dinner

W 1 Coconut Tilapia	351	9.6	30	16
1 Medium Sweet Potato, Baked	103	.2	2.3	23.6
2 Tablespoons Regular Sour Cream	51	5	.8	1

Totals	**1473**	**31.6**	**101.2**	**175.9**
GOAL	**1500**	**41.7**	**93.7**	**187.5**

1,500 Calorie - All Foods
25% Protein, 25% Fat, 50% Carbohydrates
6 Day Plan (Day 5)

Breakfast

	Cal	Fat	Pro	Carb
W 1 Whole Wheat Egg and Cream Cheese Casserole	422	10.5	29	50

Mid Morning Snack

	Cal	Fat	Pro	Carb
W 1 Pear Protein Bar	274	8	15	38

Lunch

	Cal	Fat	Pro	Carb
W Clam Chowder	279	2	23	41.2

Afternoon Snack

	Cal	Fat	Pro	Carb
1 Cup Kashi GoLEAN Crunch! Honey Almond Flax	200	5	9	34

Dinner

	Cal	Fat	Pro	Carb
W 1 Baked Chicken Chimichanga	414	9.5	33	47

	Cal	Fat	Pro	Carb
Totals	1589	35	109	210.2
GOAL	1500	41.7	93.7	187.5

1,500 Calorie - All Foods
25% Protein, 25% Fat, 50% Carbohydrates
6 Day Plan (Day 6)

Breakfast

	Cal	Fat	Pro	Carb
2 Packets Quaker Weight Control Maple & Brown Sugar Oatmeal	320	6	14	58
1 cup Fat-free Milk	91	.6	8.7	12.3

Mid Morning Snack

1 Large Peach (5.5 oz.)	61	.4	1.4	15.5

Lunch

W Cherry Chicken Salad	330	6.5	24	50

Afternoon Snack

W 1 Chocolate Pecan Bar	225	5.7	17	30

Dinner

W 1 Sweet & Sour Beef - Crock Pot	533	16.6	65	26

	Cal	Fat	Pro	Carb
Totals	1560	35.8	130.2	191.8
GOAL	1500	41.7	93.7	187.5

1,200 Calorie - Vegetarian
25% Protein, 25% Fat, 50% Carbohydrates
6 Day Plan (Day 1)

Breakfast

	Cal	Fat	Pro	Carb
1 cup (8 oz.) 1% Low-Fat Milk	105	2.4	8.5	12.2
1 packet (1.6 oz.) Quaker Weight Control Instant Oatmeal	160	3	7	29

Mid Morning Snack

	Cal	Fat	Pro	Carb
W 1/2 Carrot Cake Protein Bar (Vegetarian)	128	1.5	8	21.5

Lunch

	Cal	Fat	Pro	Carb
W 1 Tofu, Lettuce and Tomato Sandwich	364	10	19	48

Afternoon Snack

	Cal	Fat	Pro	Carb
5 Flowerets of Cauliflower	16	.1	1.3	3.4
5 Cherry Tomatoes	25	0	0	5
2 Tablespoons Kraft Fat Free Italian	15	0	0	3

Dinner

	Cal	Fat	Pro	Carb
W 1 Spinach and Mushroom Lasagna (Crock Pot)	423	13	27	46

	Cal	Fat	Pro	Carb
Totals	1237	29.9	70.8	168.1
GOAL	1200	33.3	75	150

1,200 Calorie - Vegetarian
25% Protein, 25% Fat, 50% Carbohydrates
6 Day Plan (Day 2)

Breakfast

	Cal	Fat	Pro	Carb
1 cup (8 oz.) Fat Free (Skim) Milk	91	.6	8.7	12.3
W 1 Cornbread Red Pepper Breakfast Muffin	292	5.7	15.5	43

Mid Morning Snack

15 Almonds, Raw and Unsalted	104	9.1	3.8	3.6

Lunch

W 1 Serving of Tomato & Tofu Soup	165	2.7	9	26
1/2 Medium Apple	47	.2	.2	12.6

Afternoon Snack

W 1 Zucchini Protein Bar (Vegetarian)	228	3	16	37

Dinner

W 1 1/2 Servings Eggplant and Cauliflower Stew	314	9.9	13	46.5

Totals	**1241**	**31.2**	**66.4**	**180.9**
GOAL	**1200**	**33.3**	**75**	**150**

1,200 Calorie - Vegetarian
25% Protein, 25% Fat, 50% Carbohydrates
6 Day Plan (Day 3)

Breakfast

	Cal	Fat	Pro	Carb
2 Patties (1.3 oz.) Morningstar Farms Vegetarian Sausage	160	6	20	6
W 1 Cottage Cheese Cereal	186	.2	22	25

Mid Morning Snack

	Cal	Fat	Pro	Carb
W 1/2 Honey Coconut Peanut Butter Fiber Bar	184	5	7	33.5

Lunch

	Cal	Fat	Pro	Carb
W 1 Peanut Butter & Jelly Sandwich	342	11	17.5	54

Afternoon Snack

	Cal	Fat	Pro	Carb
15 Medium Baby Carrots	52	.2	1	12.4

Dinner

	Cal	Fat	Pro	Carb
W 6 Vegan Italian Meatless Balls	291	7.5	23	37
W 1/2 Cup Vegan Italian Meatless Balls Tomato Topping	30	0	1	5

	Cal	Fat	Pro	Carb
Totals	**1246**	**29.9**	**91.5**	**172.9**
GOAL	**1200**	**33.3**	**75**	**150**

1,200 Calorie - Vegetarian
25% Protein, 25% Fat, 50% Carbohydrates
6 Day Plan (Day 4)

Breakfast

	Cal	Fat	Pro	Carb
W 2 Strawberry Protein Waffles	280	3	17	53

Mid Morning Snack

	Cal	Fat	Pro	Carb
15-20 Walnut Halves, Raw, Unsalted	176	16.8	6.8	2.8

Lunch

	Cal	Fat	Pro	Carb
W 1 Pumpkin and Black Bean Soup (Vegetarian)	163	1	7	31
2 Patties of Morningstar Farms Vegetarian Chik'n Grillers	160	6	18	14

Afternoon Snack

	Cal	Fat	Pro	Carb
W 1 No Lettuce Salad (With Feta Cheese)	141	3.6	9	21

Dinner

	Cal	Fat	Pro	Carb
1 Slice of 100% Whole Wheat Nature's Own Bread	60	1	4	11
W 1 Serving Eggplant Casserole	212	4	9.5	38

	Cal	Fat	Pro	Carb
Totals	1192	35.4	71.3	170.8
GOAL	1200	33.3	75	150

1,200 Calorie - Vegetarian
25% Protein, 25% Fat, 50% Carbohydrates
6 Day Plan (Day 5)

Breakfast

	Cal	Fat	Pro	Carb
W 1 Serving Crock Pot Oatmeal / No Half & Half	318	10	7	48

Mid Morning Snack

	Cal	Fat	Pro	Carb
W 1/2 Strawberry Cheesecake Protein Shake	116	3.2	9.5	13.5

Lunch

	Cal	Fat	Pro	Carb
W 1 Serving of Tomato & Tofu Soup	165	2.7	9	26
W 1 Vegetable & Fruit Cupcake (Vegetarian)	93	2.4	3.3	15

Afternoon Snack

	Cal	Fat	Pro	Carb
W 1 Cucumber Caramel Shake	369	2.4	36	51

Dinner

	Cal	Fat	Pro	Carb
W 1 Serving Veggie Stack	188	6	10	29

	Cal	Fat	Pro	Carb
Totals	**1250**	**26.8**	**74.8**	**182.5**
GOAL	**1200**	**33.3**	**75**	**150**

1,200 Calorie - Vegetarian
25% Protein, 25% Fat, 50% Carbohydrates
6 Day Plan (Day 6)

Breakfast

	Cal	Fat	Pro	Carb
1 cup Fiber One Honey Clusters Cereal ...	160	1.5	5	42
1 cup (8 oz.) Fat Free (Skim) Milk	91	.6	8.7	12.3

Mid Morning Snack

12 Almonds, Raw, Unsalted	83	7.3	3.1	2.8

Lunch

W 1/2 Serving Broccoli & Pine Nut Salad	180	7.5	16	24.5
W 1 White Chocolate and Vanilla Protein Pudding	120	1	6	13

Afternoon Snack

W 1 Coconut Apple Loaf	244	2.6	18	38

Dinner

W 1 Slice (1/4 of Pizza) Vegetarian Pizza with Boboli Crust	368	6	20	58

Totals	**1246**	**26.5**	**76.8**	**190.5**
GOAL	**1200**	**33.3**	**75**	**150**

1,500 Calorie - Vegetarian
25% Protein, 25% Fat, 50% Carbohydrates
6 Day Plan (Day 1)

Breakfast

	Cal	Fat	Pro	Carb
1 cup (8 oz.) 1% Low-Fat Milk	105	2.4	8.5	12.2
1 packet (1.6 oz.) Quaker Weight Control Instant Oatmeal	160	3	7	29

Mid Morning Snack

	Cal	Fat	Pro	Carb
W 1 Carrot Cake Protein Bar (Vegetarian)	257	3	16	43
12 Almonds, Raw, Unsalted	83	7.3	3.1	2.8

Lunch

	Cal	Fat	Pro	Carb
W 1 Tofu, Lettuce and Tomato Sandwich	364	10	19	48

Afternoon Snack

	Cal	Fat	Pro	Carb
8 Flowerets of Cauliflowers	26	.1	2.1	5.5
8 Cherry Tomatoes	40	0	0	8
3 Tablespoons Kraft Fat Free Italian	22	0	0	4.5

Dinner

	Cal	Fat	Pro	Carb
W 1 Spinach and Mushroom Lasagna (Crock Pot)	423	13	27	46

	Cal	Fat	Pro	Carb
Totals	**1481**	**38.8**	**82.6**	**199**
GOAL	**1500**	**41.7**	**93.7**	**187.5**

1,500 Calorie - Vegetarian
25% Protein, 25% Fat, 50% Carbohydrates
6 Day Plan (Day 2)

Breakfast

	Cal	Fat	Pro	Carb
2 cups (8 oz. each) 1% Low-Fat Milk 211	4.8	17.1	24.4
W 1 Cornbread Red Pepper Breakfast Muffin 292	5.7	15.5	43

Mid Morning Snack

15 Almonds, Raw and Unsalted 104	9.1	3.8	3.6
W 1 Chocolate Chip Brownie with Caramel Frosting 180	3	8	31

Lunch

W 1 Serving of Tomato & Tofu Soup 165	2.7	9	26
1/2 Medium Apple 47	.2	.2	12.6

Afternoon Snack

W 1 Zucchini Protein Bar (Vegetarian) 228	3	16	37

Dinner

W 1 1/2 Servings Eggplant and Cauliflower Stew 314	9.9	13	46.5

Totals	**1541**	**38.3**	**82.7**	**224**
GOAL	**1500**	**41.7**	**93.7**	**187.5**

1,500 Calorie - Vegetarian
25% Protein, 25% Fat, 50% Carbohydrates
6 Day Plan (Day 3)

Breakfast

	Cal	Fat	Pro	Carb
2 Patties (1.3 oz.) Morningstar Farms Vegetarian Sausage	160	6	20	6
W 1 Cottage Cheese Cereal	186	.2	22	25

Mid Morning Snack

	Cal	Fat	Pro	Carb
W 1 Honey Coconut Peanut Butter Fiber Bar	369	10	14	67

Lunch

	Cal	Fat	Pro	Carb
W 1 Peanut Butter & Jelly Sandwich	342	11	17.5	54

Afternoon Snack

	Cal	Fat	Pro	Carb
15 Medium Baby Carrots	52	.2	1	12.4

Dinner

	Cal	Fat	Pro	Carb
W 6 Vegan Italian Meatless Balls	291	7.5	23	37
W 1/2 Cup Vegan Italian Meatless Balls Tomato Topping	30	0	1	5

	Cal	Fat	Pro	Carb
Totals	**1430**	**34.9**	**98.5**	**206.4**
GOAL	**1500**	**41.7**	**93.7**	**187.5**

1,500 Calorie - Vegetarian
25% Protein, 25% Fat, 50% Carbohydrates
6 Day Plan (Day 4)

Breakfast

	Cal	Fat	Pro	Carb
1 cup (8 oz.) 1% Low-Fat Milk	105	2.4	8.5	12.2
W 2 Strawberry Protein Waffles	280	3	17	53

Mid Morning Snack

	Cal	Fat	Pro	Carb
1/2 Blueberry Almond Protein Bar	134	3.6	6.5	23
15-20 Walnut Halves, Raw, Unsalted	176	16.8	6.8	2.8

Lunch

	Cal	Fat	Pro	Carb
W 1 Pumpkin and Black Bean Soup (Vegetarian)	163	1	7	31
2 Patties of Morningstar Farms Vegetarian Chik'n Grillers	160	6	18	14

Afternoon Snack

	Cal	Fat	Pro	Carb
W 1 No Lettuce Salad (With Feta Cheese)	141	3.6	9	21

Dinner

	Cal	Fat	Pro	Carb
1 Slice of 100% Whole Wheat Nature's Own Bread	60	1	4	11
W 1 Serving Eggplant Casserole	212	4	9.5	38

	Cal	Fat	Pro	Carb
Totals	**1431**	**41.3**	**86.4**	**206**
GOAL	**1500**	**41.7**	**93.7**	**187.5**

1,500 Calorie - Vegetarian
25% Protein, 25% Fat, 50% Carbohydrates
6 Day Plan (Day 5)

Breakfast

	Cal	Fat	Pro	Carb
W 1 Serving Crock Pot Oatmeal / No Half & Half	318	10	7	48

Mid Morning Snack

	Cal	Fat	Pro	Carb
W 1 Strawberry Cheesecake Protein Shake	233	6.5	19	27

Lunch

	Cal	Fat	Pro	Carb
W 1 Serving of Tomato & Tofu Soup	165	2.7	9	26
W 1 Vegetable & Fruit Cupcake (Vegetarian)	93	2.4	3.3	15

Afternoon Snack

	Cal	Fat	Pro	Carb
W 1 Cucumber Caramel Shake	369	2.4	36	51

Dinner

	Cal	Fat	Pro	Carb
W 1 Serving Veggie Stack	188	6	10	29
1 cup (8 oz.) 1% Low-Fat Milk	105	2.4	8.5	12.2
Totals	**1471**	**32.4**	**92.8**	**208.3**
GOAL	**1500**	**41.7**	**93.7**	**187.5**

1,500 Calorie - Vegetarian
25% Protein, 25% Fat, 50% Carbohydrates
6 Day Plan (Day 6)

Breakfast

	Cal	Fat	Pro	Carb
1 cup Fiber One Honey Clusters Cereal ...	160	1.5	5	42
1 cup (8 oz.) 1% Low-Fat Milk	105	2.4	8.5	12.2

Mid Morning Snack

	Cal	Fat	Pro	Carb
20 Almonds, Raw, Unsalted	139	12.2	5.1	4.7
W 1/2 Cucumber Caramel Shake	184	1.2	18	25.5

Lunch

	Cal	Fat	Pro	Carb
W 1/2 Serving Broccoli & Pine Nut Salad	180	7.5	16	24.5
W 1 White Chocolate and Vanilla Protein Pudding	120	1	6	13

Afternoon Snack

	Cal	Fat	Pro	Carb
W 1 Coconut Apple Loaf	244	2.6	18	38

Dinner

	Cal	Fat	Pro	Carb
W 1 Slice (1/4 of Pizza) Vegetarian Pizza with Boboli Crust	368	6	20	58

	Cal	Fat	Pro	Carb
Totals	**1501**	**34.3**	**96.6**	**217.9**
GOAL	**1500**	**41.7**	**93.7**	**187.5**

Shopping Strategy

Modern supermarkets are amazing places. Some have produce sections that feel like a rainforest, baked goods sections that look like you've stepped back in time to 19th-century Europe and almost all have music piped in to relax you. A typical store carries 30,000 to 40,000, mostly perishable products, carefully arranged to make you want to buy.

The grocery store is in business to make a profit and there's nothing wrong with them putting you at ease so you spend more money. But that doesn't mean you have to splurge on empty calories. Here's how to get what you need, not what they want to sell you.

What to do at Home

Your first step is to make a menu of what you're going to eat. If you read the last two chapters, you've got that menu. If you don't, go back and make it before you do anything else. Then, make a list based on your menu.

Go through your kitchen and make note of the things you already have. Only put the items you need on the list. It's a shocking statistic, but according to Timothy W. Jones, an anthropologist at the University of Arizona, Americans throw away nearly half of everything they buy. If you don't need it for your menu plan, don't put it on the list.

Next, map out your trip. Many stores offer maps showing where things are located. If you can get one, group the things on your list so you get through the store as quickly as possible. Time is important because supermarkets know the longer you stay in the store, the more money you're likely to spend. Don't walk down aisles unless you're going to purchase something in them.

Be sure to eat something before you shop. You've probably heard that dozens of times before, but this is why it's so important. Good smells sell. When you walk into a grocery store, you're often surrounded by the aroma of freshly baked bread. That smell can trigger hunger pangs and a desire to buy junk food. If you've eaten, you're more likely to resist that temptation.

Grab reusable shopping bags. You'll have less plastic to throw away when you get home and some stores will even give you credit for each bag of your own you use.

Plan Your Trip Through the Store

Start by walking past the specials at the entrance. The supermarkets know you're more likely to spend money at the beginning of your trip than the end, which is why candy, plants, wines and other promotional items crowd the front door. They know your resistance is lower and you're more likely to put them in the cart. Ignore the specials and walk to the things on your list. If you want to check out the sales, do it at the end of your trip while you're waiting in line to check-out.

Shop from the right side of the store and move to your left. The majority of people are right-handed and are inclined to move from left to right. That's why stores put their most frequently visited departments furthest from the entrance. They often design a right hand loop pattern that passes you by the specials and high profit items first. It's the long way through the store.

If you start on the right and move left, you'll get the essentials you need more quickly. Remember, the less time you spend in the store, the less likely it is you'll buy junk food you don't need.

Skip the aisles in the middle of the store. The freshest and healthiest merchandise almost always lies around the edges. They put the fresh stuff there because it's easier to restock the perimeter on a daily or weekly basis. Only venture into the inner aisles for items on your list.

Produce departments are often near the beginning of your trip and they're designed to lure you in. Beautiful flowers, plump ripe fruits and gorgeous vegetables are laid out to give you a sense of "health and freshness." Since you're more likely to buy things at the beginning of your shopping trip, you're shown the most perishable and profitable stuff first. When people leave that section, they feel less guilt about grabbing soda, cookies, chips and candies. Stick to your list.

Fruits and Vegetables

If you want to save some money, choose whole fruits and vegetables instead of pre-cut. You also lower the risk of cross contamination that can occur when commercial kitchens slice up large volumes of produce together. If you're in a hurry and decide to buy the pre-packaged salads, look for ones that have at least seven days before they expire.

When Consumers Union tested packaged salads, the closer they were to expiring, the higher the levels of enterococcus and coliform bacteria were. Rewash everything, even bags that claim they were "triple washed."

As you're moving down your list, write down the cost of produce when you pick it up. More mistakes happen with produce than any other item in the store. When merchandise doesn't have a bar code, it's easier for a busy clerk to enter the numbers or quantities incorrectly. You don't want to buy something that charges per unit (like a head of lettuce) and instead be charged that same price per pound.

Cereals, Oatmeals and Private Labels

You'll find the healthiest options up high. Products placed at eye level sell better than similar products higher or lower. In the cereal aisle the brightly colored, sugar filled disasters tend to be on the bottom shelves where kids will grab them while singing the refrain of "can I have this, can I have this?" The higher fiber and lower sugar options are more often across the top shelves. Also don't bother expecting anything to be in alphabetical order.

Forcing you to look through them all leads to higher sales from impulse buys.

If you do have kids along, use them to help you find the best. Tell them they can get any cereal that has six grams of sugar or less per serving. Then, show them where they can find that on the label. It teaches them how to read the label and pay attention to what's in their food.

Compare the newer brands to older ones. New doesn't necessarily make it better or healthier. Look at regular Cheerios beside Multi-Grain Cheerios. The old regular is much lower in sugar and the Multi-Grain doesn't offer any additional fiber.

Be careful of pre-packaged oatmeals. Don't settle for brands that advertise "Lower Sugar." Instead, look for brands that have no sugar. Your best buys are the large containers of rolled oats, but they don't have the flavorings. However, you can add things like cinnamon, fresh sliced fruit, or sugar free maple syrup. If you want something a little more firm, choose steel cut oats. Keep in mind, traditional steel cut can take 25-30 minutes to cook, so they might not be a good choice if you're in a hurry.

Spices, Syrups and Dressings

Small is beautiful when it comes to seasonings. The average spice will lose much of its flavor after sitting on a shelf for two years. Buying big jars you end up throwing away is just a waste. Little jars are good, pouches may be enough, or you might even get all the seasonings you need in multi-spice packs so nothing goes to waste. Always check to confirm you're getting the lower sodium versions.

Syrup toppings are wonderful, but look for the sugar free varieties. If you're really concerned about "natural," only buy the ones that say "pure maple syrup." The rest are primarily sugar, colorings and water.

Choose lowfat or fat free dressings to make raw vegetables taste great. The low-fat typically have less sodium and sugar than the fat free, so you need to balance out what's more important for you; reducing the fat, the salt or the sugar.

Breads and Snack Bars

When you buy bread, it doesn't matter how many grains are in a loaf. More grains don't make it more healthy. One of the biggest benefits of bread is the fiber. In order to find the highest fiber content, look for the words "Whole Wheat" on the label. A reasonable choice has three grams of fiber per slice. Keep in mind that phrases "enriched wheat" and "white wheat" are not the same as whole wheat.

Snack or Nutrition Bars are terrible choices. Most are high in sugar, simple carbs, fat and sodium but low in protein. These are often just candy bars in healthier food wrappings. If you want snack bars, go to the protein bar section of www.WeCookFit.com and make your own.

Eggs and Milk

To get the freshest eggs, don't look for the "use by" date on the side. Instead, look for the number that's between 001 and 365. That number stands for the day it was packaged. 001 is January 1st and 365 is December 31st. You can often find a range of more than a month between the newest and oldest eggs. While you're looking at eggs, don't bother getting ones with colored shells unless it's Easter and you're feeling uninspired. Brown shelled eggs are the same nutritionally as white eggs, they just cost more.

Be cautious when choosing cartons of egg whites. They're often more expensive than whole eggs you have to separate and many have extra sodium added.

Milk is a staple, but you should only choose 1% or fat free. What many people don't realize is 2% milk gets 36% of it's calories from fat. When milk drinkers were blindfolded and asked to sample milk one step leaner than they usually drank, most couldn't tell a difference. Move down one level and save the fat.

While you're at it, always check out the lowest racks of milk for the freshest product. People often look in the back, but they rarely look down.

Meats

In the meat section, leaner is better. Steaks with the name "round" or "chuck" are going to have the lowest fat. Choose 94% lean or greater for ground beef and 98% lean or greater for ground turkey. When you buy chicken get it without the skin and remember that white meat is lower in fat than dark meat. There are even lower fat cuts of pork.

Don't skip the less traditional options. Buffalo, reindeer, moose and ostrich meats are all available and often both lean and tasty.

Remember to buy fish. They're packed with protein and many have healthy fats that help your heart. When you're deciding how much you need, a typical meat serving is the size of a pack of cards.

Save More Money

Be skeptical of Half Off sales. It's not unusual for supermarkets to take an item, double the price for a week, and then put it on sale for half off.

Write down the prices of sale items. A person has to change the price in the computer from regular to the sale price. Whenever a human is involved, mistakes are possible. Watch as the sale items are rung up and compare them to what you wrote down on your shopping list.

When comparing two items, always check the package weight, not just the size. Companies are reluctant to raise prices, so instead, what they often do is reduce how much is included in the package. Coffee is a classic example. In the past, tin cans held a pound (16 oz.) of coffee. Today they hold 12 ounces or less.

Endcaps or end-of-aisle displays don't always feature sale items. They're considered prime selling locations because customers pass by them more frequently, so stores use them for a variety of purposes including introducing new products or clearing out slow moving merchandise. If it's not on your list, you're probably safe ignoring it.

Skip the bottled water aisle. If you want the convenience, get some washable bottles, put a filter on your tap and make your own. You'll save money, plus reduce your environmental impact. Keep a case or two of bottled water around for emergencies only.

Consider convenience stores for quick purchases. The two most common items bought in a grocery store are bread and milk. They're often strategically placed at opposite ends of the store. To get those two items, you have to pass by thousands of other products in a maze including the rainforest produce section and cobbled streets of the bakery, laid out to slow down and entice you. Odds are while you're getting them, you're going to see at least one or two other impulse items that will end up in your basket. Avoid temptation and grab single items from a local mini-market.

Non-food items may cost more. Impulse buys like toothbrushes, shampoos, paper and light bulbs are often more expensive in grocery stores versus drug, office supply or hardware stores. Pick them up if you want to save some time, but if you want to save money, you can generally get them for less at other places.

TAKE ACTION:
The next time you go shopping, make a promise not to buy anything that isn't on your menu or list.

Summary
Shopping Strategy

Make a Plan

Start with a menu, make a list, get your bags and map your way through the store.

Shop the Edges

Stick to the edges of the store, that's where the freshest and healthiest items are found. Only venture into inner aisles for specific items on your list. Don't "browse" those aisles.

Take Your Time

The first few times you shop, after you start reading labels, it's going to take longer. Plan on spending 50% more time. Once you identify the healthiest versions, future shopping trips won't take nearly as long.

Kitchen Makeover

Many modern kitchens have turned into a dumping ground. Instead of a pleasant environment where healthy foods are prepared; they've become a place to store the remnants of impulse purchases and takeout food, with high calorie and fatty snacks lurking in every corner and cupboard.

If yours is like that, don't let it stay that way. Resolve to turn your kitchen into a junk-free oasis. You want a nice welcome environment to prepare healthy meals in. Start by thoroughly cleaning it from top to bottom.

Then make sure you have at least two non-stick frying pans, one non-stick or cast iron pot for stews or soups and another pot for boiling water. Traditional pots are OK, but the non-stick varieties require less butter or oils when you're cooking. They're also easier to cleanup, so that won't be a deterrent to healthier cooking, or an excuse to eat out.

Make sure you have a steamer basket. It should fit on top of one of the pots you boil water in. It's a quick and easy way to prepare vegetables. While you're at it make sure you have a colander to rinse things off.

If you don't have one, pickup a 9 x 13 inch dish for baking. Then check your cookie sheet. If it's black and burnt or losing it's non-stick coating, it's time to replace it. Several dishes you can bake instead of frying to reduce the fat. A mini loaf pan for homemade protein bars is handy too.

You should also have two cutting boards. One for vegetables and one for meat to prevent cross-contamination.

Keep a decorative bowl on the counter for fresh fruit. Make sure to put it someplace prominent so you see it and actually eat the fruit. If you eat a lot of bananas, a banana tree will help prevent bruising.

Come home to a hot meal by using a crock pot (also known as a slow cooker). You can fill it full of meat, vegetables and spices before you leave for the day, and when you return you'll have a fresh cooked homemade meal. Then put the leftovers in individual serving containers and freeze them for another day.

Toss out the full fat condiments, regular mayonnaise, full fat salad dressings and any jar or canned cheeses. They're subtle but effective diet-killers. Replace them with low-fat or fat-free salad dressings and mayonnaise. Mustard, barbecue sauce and low sodium teriyaki sauces can also be good choices.

Replace traditional jellies and jams with the low or sugar free versions. Buy natural peanut butters that don't add extra sugar or large amounts of salt.

Put baking ingredients in airtight containers. Keep the bugs out and the freshness in.

Spices and herbs make food more interesting. Don't be afraid to experiment with something exotic. Try a little basil, curry, orange peel, rosemary, sage or thyme in your food. Once a month choose a new herb or spice to sample. You'll find new ways to enjoy old foods without always resorting to salt, butter or fat on top.

Give away any bags of chips, boxes of cookies or tubs of ice cream. These are the potholes on the road to health. If you find it hard to resist temptation, get rid of the tempting foods that are nutritionally empty. When you want a treat, leave your house to get it and only buy a single serving.

If you insist on keeping junk food around, limit yourself to just one thing. When there are several cheats to choose from you're more likely to find one you'll give in to.

Stock up on fruits and vegetables, but purchase frozen ones that have nothing added. Frozen foods won't go bad as quickly as fresh vegetables do, so you can always have some on hand. You also save money because you won't be throwing away spoiled produce. If you prefer canned foods, make sure to get the no salt and no sugar added varieties.

If you're cooking for one or two, separate foods destined for the freezer into individual portions. You can still save money buying that economy sized package of meat, but with everything individually wrapped you only have to defrost what you plan to eat.

Print out good recipes and put healthy cookbooks out in the open. Set aside an hour or two once a week to prepare something special that's also good for you.

Finally, post a picture of your goal on the refrigerator. It'll remind you why you're making responsible eating choices.

TAKE ACTION:
Schedule a date and time when you'll be cleaning out your kitchen. Do it before your next shopping trip.

Summary
Kitchen Makeover

Clean

Clean your kitchen from top to bottom and throw out the diet destroyers. Your kitchen should be an oasis of healthy choices.

Get the Tools

Buy the pots, pans and utensils that will help you prepare the foods you should be eating.

Make Time to Cook

Put specific days and times on your calendar when you'll be preparing your food. If you don't put it on your schedule, it probably won't happen.

Refrigerator Makeover

A big obstacle to healthy eating may be with one of your major appliances. In this section, you'll learn how to enlist your refrigerator to be part of your support system. It doesn't take long, but if you follow these simple suggestions you'll have some of the freshest and healthiest food around.

Each number corresponds to a specific location in the refrigerator. You can see the illustration on the next page.

1. Move fruits and vegetables out of the crisper to the top shelf. Americans waste millions of dollars every week on food that spoils before it can be eaten. Produce should be the first thing you see, not shoved in a drawer that rarely gets opened.

Put produce in plastic bags where they can stay slightly moist (not wet). Don't wash them until just before you eat because wet produce grows mold more easily.

2. Keep your eggs in a carton, not in the refrigerator door. Eggs kept in the door will go bad faster from the changing temperature every time you open and close the door.

3. Put healthy, single-serving snacks (like a sugar-free protein pudding or low-fat cottage cheese) at eye level. When you're hungry for a quick bite these should be the easiest things to reach.

4. Put lunchmeat in airtight containers, not the bags provided by the deli counter. Buy cold cuts freshly sliced so you can choose ones that have less sodium than the pre-packaged brands.

Lunchmeat is bad if it smells sweet or has a slippery coating.

The Diet is Dead

5. Keep plenty of milk on hand, but not whole milk. Milk is loaded with vitamin D and calcium. Skim has the fewest calories but 1% is reasonable as well.

6. Make sugar free drinks, tea and have pitchers of water. Keep them easily accessible.

7. Store fresh meat on the lowest shelf of the refrigerator where there is no chance of it dripping onto other foods. Wrap it tightly to keep air out and juices in. If you haven't eaten the meat within 24 hours put it in the freezer so it won't go bad.

8. Candy, soda, beer and other cheat foods should be kept in the crisper. If it's out of sight you're less likely to think about or reach for it when you have a craving.

9. Go through your refrigerator door and replace the full fat foods with healthier alternatives. Fat free cream cheese, sugar free syrup and -- if you must have butter -- choose a brand that doesn't have any trans-fats. Throw away anything that has passed its expiration date.

Additional Tips

Refrigerate leftovers in clear, single serving plastic containers. Never use foil because it doesn't seal as well and you might forget what food you wrapped up. Don't put anything in that isn't covered because the smell can circulate and taint things like the ice in your freezer.

Keep healthier foods up front and less healthy options in the back.

Make healthy food more appealing. Store mixed nuts with low-fat yogurt or chocolate milk mix beside the skim milk. An indulgent topping (when used sparingly) can make healthier eating easier.

Freeze foods in individual portions to make thawing and preparing them easier. The recommended serving of cooked meat is three ounces (about the size of a deck of playing cards). A standard serving of pasta is one cup and vegetables is half a cup.

Freeze fruit for a treat. Frozen bananas, grapes and orange slices are great alternatives to ice cream.

Make sure your refrigerator is set at 34 to 40 degrees Fahrenheit (4 degrees Celsius) and your freezer is set at zero degrees Fahrenheit (-18 degrees Celsius) or less. These temperatures help prevent the growth of microorganisms that can cause food to spoil.

At least once every three months, go through your refrigerator and clean it out. Get rid of the old food that's bad or you'll never eat and make room for healthy things you will.

Keep a running list of what you need on the refrigerator door, and take it with you when you go to the grocery store so you know exactly what to buy.

If you don't eat enough fruits and vegetables, buy pre-cut ones. Yes it's more expensive, but if they're already cut up you're more likely to eat them before they spoil and that's certainly cheaper than throwing away rotten food every week.

Once you've made these minor adjustments, your refrigerator will be an ally you can rely on.

TAKE ACTION:
Schedule a date and time when you'll be cleaning out your refrigerator. Do it before your next shopping trip.

Summary
Refrigerator Makeover

Move Things Around

Move the healthy stuff to the top shelves, front and center. Put the unhealthy things in the crisper drawers or move them to the back.

Preserve It

Properly seal food so it doesn't go bad. Invest in clear containers so you can see the leftovers. You're more likely to eat what you can see.

Keep Things Clean

Put cleaning the refrigerator on a regular schedule. Keep it stocked with fresh food that's appealing to eat.

Coping Strategies

The next few chapters are strategies to deal with special events or when you're not in the safety of your own home. These are the things you should do before you go to a party, how to prepare for the holidays, what you can eat out and how to order in.

Read them now to get your mind thinking. Then read them again before the party or event.

Eating Out
Coping Strategies

When I was young, going out to eat was a special occasion. Every couple of weeks, usually on a Sunday or when relatives were visiting, we would get dressed up and go out, under strict instructions to be on our best behavior. I was always excited because it was a chance to indulge!

Fast-forward 30 years. In 2010 eating out has become a way of life. Americans consume around one third of their calories away from home in restaurants and other food-service establishments. Going out to eat isn't for special occasions anymore. For many people it's a daily occurrence.

That can be a problem.

When you buy food at the supermarket, the nutritional content is on the package. You don't have to buy the healthier foods, but if you want to, the information is there. No such luck in most restaurants.

Many restaurants (local and chains) have 1,500 calorie appetizers, 2,000 calorie entrees and 1,200 calorie desserts. For some people that's as many calories as they should eat in three days, not one meal! And the serving sizes keep growing larger.

Instead of competing to make things healthier, restaurants are trying to see who can make the most extreme meals. A lean entree doesn't make the news, but if you serve a ten pound hamburger, that gets featured on CNN. Indulgence is part of the mindset when going out, and there's an assumption that you didn't get your money's worth if your pants still fit properly after the meal. But, there's another reason too: Laziness.

It's more difficult to make a meal that's healthy AND tastes good. I know, because I work with talented chefs every week to put healthier and flavorful meals on my website. It's easy to add sugars, salt and fat to elevate an uninspired dish, and it seems far too many chefs have chosen the easy way. It is much more challenging to work with herbs, spices and creatively prepare food that people want to keep coming back for, so they go back to the default of adding to the size of the portion to give the illusion of value. What the restaurants won't do for you, you have to do for yourself.

Choosing the Restaurant

If you're serious about eating better, start with where you go out to dinner. Pick up the phone book and see if it has a section with menus in it (many do). Look and see if any of the menus offer low-calorie or healthy options. If they do, you've got a winner.

If you can't find the information in a phone book or online, give the restaurant a call before you make a reservation. Explain that one of the people who will be joining you is on a special diet, and if it would be possible to prepare the food without butter or oils. If they can, make a reservation. If they don't, ask them to recommend a place that would or look for someplace else.

Watch what you eat before you head out. Have a lighter breakfast and lunch, so you can eat more calories for dinner. Then just before you leave, eat a healthy snack so you don't go into the restaurant hungry and overindulge. A handful of dry roasted, unsalted nuts or a piece of fruit are both options.

If you're out and get hungry, read the menu posted outside to see what they have before you go in. If you go someplace regularly, see if they'll accommodate you with a special request.

Don't be afraid to vote with your feet. Recently I was at a local restaurant with a group of friends who were visiting. We sat down and read the menu, but couldn't find anything that seemed even remotely low in calories. So I asked the chef if he had any healthy options. He said, "No, people don't come here to eat healthy." My friends and I closed our menus, stood up and walked out. He doesn't have to cater to me, but I don't have to spend my money there.

Remember that your servers are just that, there to serve you. Don't be intimidated or worry that you're holding them up with your questions. You're paying the server to get the proper information to the kitchen so you can have a healthier dining experience. But the courtesy goes both ways. If a server delivers for you, make sure to tip accordingly, 20 to 30 percent is fair if they handle all your special requests.

Ordering a Guilt Free Dinner

Sometimes, when you go out to eat, you can't choose the restaurant. It might be a friend's party, a business meeting or the only place that's convenient. Whatever the reason, once you're there, you can still make healthier choices no matter what the menu says. Here's how you can avoid some of the calorie minefields spread throughout a typical restaurant meal.

Start by not drinking your calories. Order a diet soda, sparkling water with a twist of lemon, lime or an unsweetened ice tea. Skip the mixed drinks and alcohol, because some have over 600 calories in a single serving and they can weaken your willpower when it comes to ordering healthy. (When will restaurants start offering diet orange, root beer, or dozens of other diet sodas? Why is it always Diet Coke, Diet Pepsi or ice tea?)

If someone puts a bread basket or chips down in front of you, ask them to take it away. Most chips are fried in oil and covered in salt while the breads are loaded with simple sugars. If you absolutely want bread, ask if they have any whole or multi-grain varieties. If they do, take one piece to eat and have the rest removed. Don't add any butter or oil.

Order your food a la carte (each item separately) and get exactly what you want. You may have to spend a little more, but you can combine the healthiest options into a single meal.

Say no to any appetizers that are battered, breaded, deep fried or covered in sauces. If there are healthier appetizers, consider ordering them instead of an entree. Appetizer portions are usually smaller and typically have fewer calories.

If you order a salad, watch out for what gets added to it. Cheese, meat, eggs, croutons and dressings can change a low-calorie dish into a high fat disaster. Ask for the fat-free or light dressings and get them on the side. Then, dip your fork into the dressing and spear the food. If they have a salad bar, load up on fresh fruits, vegetables or boiled eggs with the yolks removed. Avoid Caesar, chef, Greek or taco salads.

Soups that are broth or tomato-based like gazpacho, minestrone and vegetable generally have fewer calories than chowder, creamed or pureed. A serving size is usually one measured cup, but many restaurants will give you two or three cup servings. Cut back by splitting a bowl with someone else at your table. Skip soup entirely if you're trying to cut down on sodium.

When ordering side dishes, look for steamed vegetable plates. Baked potatoes without the toppings are very low in calories but they're high in simple carbs. Order sweet potatoes without toppings and you get a filling, low calorie side with complex carbs. If you're not in the mood for vegetables, ask for slices of tomato, brown rice or a serving of fresh fruit. Avoid fries, onion rings and potato chips.

Be sure you know how the chef prepares meals. The menu description might not tell you all the things that are added. Remember this simple mantra, "Grilled is good, breaded is bad." Baking, grilling, roasting and steaming are generally the healthier ways food can be prepared. Frying, deep frying and sautéing all tend to add large amounts of fat to the meal. Also, ask that the kitchen avoid brushing your food with butter or oil.

Some menus will have seniors, lunch or childrens portions that are typically smaller. Half-orders and small portions are also available at some places. See if any of those are options.

Take control of what's on your plate. This is not your family dinner table where you have to eat everything put in front of you. Order an entree and split it with someone at the table. If you don't feel comfortable doing that, ask for a to-go box before the food is even delivered. Then cut everything down the middle and bring half home, that way you get two meals for the price of one. Put the extra in your to-go box before you start to eat, or you may be tempted to overindulge. Out of sight is out of mind.

When the food arrives, trim off any visible fat before you start. You should also remove the skin from chicken, turkey or other fowl.

Condiments can be your friend. Say no to added salt but indulge in the pepper. Don't put anything on your food until after you've tasted it first. Avoid pouring sugar in your drinks. If they need to be sweeter, try combining some of the different artificial sweeteners. Skip the mayonnaise but feel free to use mustard or salsa, if they have it, as both are generally low fat or fat-free.

Start eating your meals backwards. Begin with the vegetables. Fill up with the lower calorie, higher fiber foods first, before you get to the main part of your dinner.

Slow down and stop eating when you're full. It sounds obvious, but many of us will keep eating until we get that "stuffed" feeling. If you're tempted to keep eating, ask the server to remove the plate when you're done so you have to stop.

Dessert is an indulgence. Skip it if you can, or order one and split it with everyone at the table if you must. Cups of fresh fruit or flavored coffee with skim milk are also viable options.

Healthier Options in Different Types of Restaurants

When you walk into a restaurant, you usually have a good idea what type of food they serve. A deli is likely to have a large selection of sandwiches and it's a safe bet that most Italian places will have some sort of pasta.

For each type of restaurant, there are also certain dishes they'll serve that are going to be lower in calories and fat. To help you the next time you go out, here are several common restaurant types, and what you can order from them if you're trying to have a healthier dining experience.

Breakfast

Breakfast places can be surprisingly easy. Hot or cold cereals are a good start. Order fat-free (skim) milk to drink or as a topping. Egg whites or egg substitute, scrambled together with onions, green peppers and mushrooms make a terrific high protein meal. Substitute tomato slices for the hash browns and add dry, whole grain or multi-grain toast for plenty of fiber. If you want pancakes, order whole grain if you can and say "no" to butter. Top pancakes or oatmeal with sugar-free syrup.

Chinese, Thai or Vietnamese

Chinese, Thai or Vietnamese usually have stir-fried vegetables, just ask that they prepare them with very little oil. Steamed spring rolls, Hunan, Szechuan shrimp, or chicken are all healthier options, but ask that any sauces be put on the side. Brown rice is good too. Avoid the beef, pork and deep-fried or breaded ingredients. Many foods can be steamed (ask your server) to avoid fatty oils.

Tofu is deceptive. Although it is vegetarian, regular tofu gets more than 50% of its calories from fat. Firm tofu gets over 80% of its calories from fat. Tell your server you're allergic to coconut milk and nuts so they'll leave them off.

Japanese

Japanese usually means sashimi (raw fish cut into bite sized pieces) and sushi (boiled rice shaped into bite sized pieces and topped with seafood or formed into seaweed wrapped rolls). Because sashimi is typically unadorned, it tends to be low in calories and high in protein. Sushi can be healthy too, but be careful of the rolls. Many are stuffed with cream cheese, and fried fish or battered fish. The rice is typically white and that's high in simple carbohydrates, so eat it sparingly.

If they give you chopsticks, use them. Chopsticks will force you to eat slower and you may not eat as much. Go easy on the sake wine though, one six ounce glass has 234 calories.

Deli or Sandwich Shops

Deli or Sandwich Shops have plenty of options. It's safe to choose white meat turkey or chicken breast without the skin. Top any sandwich with mustard, onions, tomatoes, lettuce, sprouts, mushrooms and peppers. Make sure to skip the mayo and put everything on whole wheat breads.

Buffets

Buffets are dangerous territory. There are often so many choices, it's hard to skip the fattier offerings. There's also the feeling that you should eat a lot to get your money's worth. If you have to eat at one, look over the food before you fill your plate. Decide what you're going to eat and stick with it. Start with a plate full of healthier salad options. If you're still hungry when you're done, go back and get vegetables that don't have added butter, oil or sauces.

Fast Food

Fast food restaurants usually offer barbecue or grilled chicken breast. Ask for the mayo to be left off. Skip the fries and onion rings and order a salad without the toppings. Don't reward yourself with a shake when you're done, many have 400 to 800 calories in a single serving.

Italian

Good Italian choices are pasta with tomato or meat sauces. If the restaurant offers whole-grain pasta, order that and get more complex carbs. Request dishes without cheese on top and ask them not to add extra oil. If you're getting a pizza, order it without cheese or oil and have them load up on the vegetables.

Mexican

Mexican places usually have vegetable or chicken fajitas. Chicken or bean burritos and chicken tacos can be healthy, but make sure they don't stuff them with cheese, sour cream and avocado. Order corn tortillas instead of flour because they're much lower in fat and sodium. Skip the refried beans if they're cooked in lard. Request they not bring the complementary chips to the table.

Seafood

Seafood Restaurants are notorious for taking something healthy (fish) and covering it in breading or frying it in oil. Pass on those options, and instead order broiled or grilled fish and baked or steamed veggies. Ask that butter be left off and use pepper or lemon for more flavor. Avoid the shellfish if you're trying to cut down on cholesterol.

These are all simple choices that help you enjoy your meal out, without forfeiting your health. Bon appetite.

TAKE ACTION:
Set aside 30 minutes to call your local restaurants and see which ones offer lower calorie meals. Make a list for the next time you dine out.

Summary
Eating Out

Before

Call ahead to see if they offer healthier choices.

Pick restaurants that allow special orders.

During

Don't eat the breads, chips or other snacks that are initially placed on the table.

Don't drink your calories. Order water or calorie free drinks.

Ask for meats that are grilled, roasted or baked.

Add vegetables that are steamed or baked.

Put all sauces and toppings on the side.

Put half your meal in a to-go container before you start. You don't have to clean your plate.

After

Split desserts or request fresh fruit.

Movie Theater
Coping Strategies

The smell of popcorn. The rows of chocolate and candy. Giant cups full of sweet soda. That's what's waiting for you every time you walk into a movie theater. The pictures of happy cartoon candy get more attention than the admonishments to silence your cell phone. Junk food is presented as a coming attraction, but available *right now* in the lobby. If you're trying to cut down on your calories, it can be a dietary debacle. Here's how to avoid all that temptation and still see the latest films.

Take control before you ever get to the theatre. Follow the same rule as before you go shopping. Eat something first, so you don't arrive hungry. If you're going to an early show, plan on what you'll eat afterward so you don't binge when you get home.

When you're ready to go, bring along a protein or low-fat granola bar to snack on during the film. You could also pack a small plastic bag of carrots, celery, orange slices or grapes. (Keep in mind some theatres don't allow outside food so this may not be an option.)

When you get to the theatre, popcorn is the most critical thing to control. Approach it like kryptonite for dieting superman or woman. If you make a bowl of microwave popcorn at home, the average serving size is two cups. It holds about 90 calories and five grams of fat. That's too much fat to be considered healthy, but with just 90 calories it's probably not going to do any kind of damage to your diet. That's not true for movie popcorn.

A small popcorn in most theatre chains holds about nine cups. That's 405 calories and 22 grams of fat. Add butter and you can easily push the calorie count past 550 calories and the fat over 30 grams. Remember, that's just a small!

Order a typical large popcorn and you're looking at 22 cups and at least 1,000 calories. Add butter and that large popcorn may end up holding 1,500 calories and more than 65 grams of fat. Three full meals in a bag, with nothing to show for it but empty calories.

As scary as that is, in the age of mega food there's always something bigger. Some theatres now offer a tub of popcorn that tops out at an astonishing 30+ cups. It's the "two-usher" size, because that's how many people it takes to get it to your seat. If you add butter, a tub can hold more than 2,000 calories and give you two full days of fat.

To make matters worse, the size of the popcorn containers entice us to eat even more. Researchers in Philadelphia randomly gave movie goers free popcorn in large and extra large containers. The people who got the extra large containers ate 45% more than those with just the large containers.

There was a twist. Half the movie goers popcorn was fresh and half was 14 days old. Incredibly, even those who received stale popcorn ate 33% more if they got it in a larger container.[21] (To be fair, it might have been fresh when they started the experiment, but those tubs are really big.)

The secret to eating less may be as simple as a small brown paper lunch bag. Here's what you do. If you can't watch a movie without popcorn, first decide how many cups it's OK for you to eat. Keep in mind each cup holds a minimum of 45 calories.

If you're with a group of friends, ask them how many cups they want. Then add up the total number of cups and buy the size popcorn that matches. Small typically holds nine cups, a medium is about 15 and a large is around 22.

---

21. Wansink B, Kim J., Department of Applied Economics and Management, Cornell University, Ithica, New York, USA.; *Bad popcorn in big buckets: portion size can influence intake as much as taste.* Journal of Nutrition, Education and Behavior 2005 Sep-Oct;37(5):242-5.

Once you've got your popcorn, all you have to do is split it up between each of the brown paper bags. The smaller bags help control your eating urges and the measured portion virtually guarantees you won't eat more than you had planned. As a bonus everyone saves money by sharing.

How you order your drink is the next challenge. In many theatres a "small" soda is a full 32 ounces. The large cups hold as much as 86 ounces. (By comparison, when you buy a can of soda you're getting 12 ounces.) If you buy a regular Coca-Cola, that 32 ounce "small" has 388 calories and nearly one and a half days of sugar...108 grams. Order the large and you're holding an unbelievable 1043 calories and 290 grams of sugar.

Step away from the regular sodas. If you want something carbonated, choose one of the diet drinks. They don't have sugar and most are calorie free. To save money, bring along some collapsible camping cups or ask the theater for complimentary glasses and split a large drink with your family and friends. Buy an extra large if you want to share with family, friends, and the rows in front of and behind you.

If you don't want soda, punch up a bottle of water. Most theatres carry bottled water, so you just have to bring along handy "to go" pouches of Crystal Light or Wylers. Pour a pouch in the bottle of water and you can have zero calorie ice tea, peach, raspberry, orange or lemonade drinks. The theatre still makes their money on the water and you get a healthier alternative to carbonated sugar filled soda.

Candy is the next hurdle. Like popcorn, the bags of candy sold at many movie theatres have been supersized. If you didn't or couldn't bring along some kind of health or protein bar, and you've got to have some candy, split it with someone. Just like you brought bags for the popcorn, carry some small plastic bags for the candy. Open the package and split it between two, three or four people so everyone gets a little to enjoy.

Make sure you're always ready. Put some brown paper bags for the popcorn, small plastic bags for the candy and collapsible cups for the soda in your car. Then, every time you head to the theatre your portion control help is right at hand.

The secret is not depriving yourself, just take a couple minutes to plan ahead. Your body will thank you and so will your wallet.

The Ugly Trans-Fat Secret

If you're lucky enough to live in a town where there's more than one theatre, here's one way you can choose which one will get your business. In 1994 the Center for Science in the Public Interest (CSPI) surveyed theatres to find out what they cooked their popcorn in. They found seven out of ten theatres used coconut oil.[22]

No problem, right? Coconut oil... you may be picturing a beach scene with palm trees swaying in a light breeze. Unfortunately, that's not what's happening in your arteries. A kid sized bag of popcorn cooked in coconut oil has 20 grams of fat, with 14 of them heart clogging saturated fat.

CSPI found that a large bag of popcorn has 80 grams of fat, 50 of them saturated. That's the same amount of saturated fat as six McDonald's Big Mac's! All of those were without the optional "buttery" topping.

News stations ran the headlines and theatres around the country started switching to heart healthier canola oil. But there's a catch. Some were using canola oil, others used canola shortening or partially hydrogenated canola oil. The difference is important.

Canola oil has no trans fat. However, when you partially hydrogenate canola oil or change it into a shortening, you introduce trans fats. Trans fats are so unhealthy there are no acceptable amounts people should eat.

So how are the theatres doing today? Contact your local theater or check on their website to see if they list what they use. If you've got a choice, choose the one that uses heart healthier canola oils first.

---

22. Juliann Goldman, Ingrid VanTuinen, Maxine Anderson, Anne Didato, and Michelle Werkstell, Center for Science in the Public Interest, Washington, D.C., USA.; *Popcorn: Oil in a Day's Work*. Nutrition Action Health Letter, May 1994 - U.S. Edition

TAKE ACTION:
Put small bags and collapsable cups to-gether for your next trip to the theater. Use them to divide up the larger portions of food and drink you buy.

Summary
Movie Theater

Planning is Key

Eat something before you go to the movie. If you're going to an early show, plan on what you'll be eating afterwards so you don't binge when you get home.

Bring along small bags and collapsible cups to divide up the monstrous servings.

If you have a choice between multiple theaters, choose the one that has healthier options like popcorn cooked in canola oil instead of coconut oil.

Parties and Holidays
Coping Strategies

Putting on pounds over the holidays is an American tradition. It starts with the twin excuses for overindulgence, Halloween and Thanksgiving. From there it's a downhill slide into December parties and the food hangover that is New Year's Day. January 1st, the Earth is 4 degrees off its axis.

You resolve to take the pounds off in January, but wouldn't it be great if you avoided the weight gain in the first place? Then you could concentrate on getting in even better shape, instead of fighting to get back to where you were just a couple months before. Here's how.

Start by avoiding temptations you create at home. If you're making a cake, cookies or something else unhealthy, keep a piece of chewing gum in your mouth. You want something that will interfere with your desire to grab a handful of chocolate chips or lick the bowl when you're done.

Don't open boxes of candy when you're alone. Bring them to work or wait until you're with a group of people. Then you can open the box, eat a piece or two and share the rest. If your friends or co-workers are watching what they eat, don't open it at all. Take the sealed box to a food bank or soup kitchen.

If you can, walk or bike to parties. It'll give you a chance to enjoy the holiday decorations and get a little exercise. If it's far enough away that you have to drive, go ahead. But find a safe place to park before you get there and walk the last mile or so.

Don't skip meals so you can "pig out" at a party. After four hours of not eating your body turns to muscle for energy, not fat. Even worse is what will happen when you show up at the party. Arrive hungry and you're much more likely to overeat and not exercise good judgment.

When you go to a party, bring something healthy to share. Then, no matter what your host has laid out, you'll still have something good to nibble on. I always put it on a gift plate. That way, if the host doesn't have any more serving platters, it's no problem to leave it behind because it's intended for them anyway. Whenever I've done this it's amazing how many guests are relieved there's something available that won't blow their diet.

Sometimes bringing a dish of your own just isn't an option. You might be heading over straight from work, the party is being catered or you don't know the host well enough to ask if they'd mind. In those cases, try the "one bite only" plan. That's where you allow yourself to eat anything that's laid out. The only catch is that you have to limit yourself to one bite per item and no more.

That doesn't mean a bite you have to unhinge your jaw for. It must be a normal bite that you chew thoroughly. If there are fifteen types of cookies, you may not take a bite of each one. A single bite from a cookie, a single bite from a cake, a single bite of candy and so on. You enjoy the flavors while still exercising portion control.

Eat vegetables whenever possible, just avoid the sauces. If there are foods like carrots, celery, baby corn, broccoli or cauliflower, eat those first.

Now let's say there's a buffet with dozens of things to sample and even restricting yourself to a single bite of each would be a caloric catastrophie. In those cases, only sample the things you don't get the rest of the year. Skip the chips and crackers but perhaps enjoy a small glass of eggnog. Make your choices special, not common.

Make a promise you won't use a plate. Don't eat any more than you can hold in one hand and definitely don't hang around the buffet table. Walk to the other side of the room so you're not near anything tempting. It can take 15 to 20 minutes before your stomach tells your brain it's full.

Skip cocktails if you can. Alcohol stimulates the appetite and can reduce your inhibitions so you're more likely to binge. Ask for non-alcoholic drinks like diet soda or unsweetened ice tea with artificial sweeteners. If people expect you to be holding a drink, get some seltzer water with a splash of lemon, lime or cranberry juice.

Want to have a drink? Go ahead, just follow each glass of alcohol with a glass of water. It'll help keep you hydrated and reduce the total calories you're taking in.

Tell your friends and loved ones you're watching your weight. You like the food, but you just want smaller portions. If you're dealing with a "food pusher" that keeps insisting you eat more, use stall tactics. Excuse yourself for a bathroom break and don't return to the table.

In the case of really aggressive hosts, you may have to slip out the bathroom window, but beware of the hosts upon whom you've tried this before. There may be cakes and cookies strategically left outside all the windows, which, on the upside will help break your fall. In reality though, in most larger gatherings, people will often forget you skipped the extra helpings.

During dinner, don't load your plate with the tastes you already know you like. Restrict yourself to sampling only unfamiliar foods. You'll expose yourself to new tastes and avoid binging on old favorites.

When dessert is being offered, politely decline and say you're full. Don't give in to food bullies. It's your body and you don't have to eat anything you don't want to. Practice saying "no thank you" and remain firm.

If your host keeps insisting, ask for it "to go" so you can enjoy it later or share with a loved one. When you get home you can dispose of it without worry of offending anyone. Then wash the plate so you can return it with a thank you note. If there are no other options and you're expected to eat a piece, ask for a small one. Enjoy the flavor and eat slowly.

After the party, get rid of the diet disasters. Foods like turkey can make great leftovers, but just make sure to dump the gravy and toss the skin. A turkey sandwich with lettuce, tomato, mustard and fat free mayo on whole wheat is a very healthy meal.

Don't be afraid to get out early. If you've gone through everything and still find yourself craving, thank the host and go home. You can't indulge if you aren't near the food.

For those of you constantly surrounded by food, start keeping a journal or notebook. Commit yourself to writing down everything you eat and drink over the holidays. It's a great way to stay accountable. You're far less likely to down a half dozen sugar cookies if you have to document it somewhere.

Not the type that likes to write? Get some Post-it notes and put one on your refrigerator for every piece of cake, candy or fatty food that's not on your healthy food plan. Keep them up for a week as a visual reminder of what you're really eating. Seeing that you "slip" four or five times a day may be the kick you need to be more careful.

Finally, don't plan on starting a diet during the holidays. Simply concentrate on not adding any extra pounds before January and consider that a great achievement.

TAKE ACTION:
Pick out a couple healthy things you can make for your next party. Ask the host if it'll be OK. If it is, make it and you'll have at least one guilt-free thing to nibble on.

Summary
Parties and Holidays

Before

Eat something before you go and prepare a healthy snack to bring and share. Walk or bike to the party if you can, otherwise park far enough away so you can get some exercise walking those last few blocks.

During

Don't eat more than a bite of anything. Don't pickup more food than you can hold in your hand. Don't hang out around the tables of food. Excuse yourself and leave when food pushers keep insisting you eat more.

After

Dump any leftovers that aren't in your diet plan. Write down everything you ate and drank. Knowing you'll be accountable can help maintain willpower.

Halloween
Coping Strategies

It's Halloween and if you're trying to lose weight, it's not the costumes that are scary. Everywhere you go you're surrounded by candy and sweets, brightly-colored and festive. Your willpower may be tested – the Goblins of gobblin' – but you can avoid going on a binge.

Start by being less responsible. Resist the urge to buy candy early. Wait until the day you need it before you buy it. The longer you have it around, the more likely you are to indulge. A bonus of "planning behind" is that many stores will have sales to try and clear out excess inventory.

Buy only as much as you need. Don't buy five large bags of candy if you only get a half dozen trick-or-treaters stopping by. Gauge your traffic by how many visited last year and shop accordingly. If you live somewhere new, ask the neighbors how many kids have visited in the past. No fair turning off your porch light just as you open the bag you really like.

Speaking of which, it's better to avoid treats you crave. If your favorite thing is chocolate bars, buy hard candy. If you're a sucker for lollipops, load up on bubble gum or chocolate. If your favorite is anything sweet, get something completely different. Purchase small toys or gifts to hand out to kids. Most probably don't need the extra sugar and fat anyway.

Look for lower calorie, pre-packaged "100 calorie" snacks to hand out. Boxes of animal crackers, individual packages of vanilla wafers or ginger snaps. Since they're already packed into lower calorie, individual servings, it may be easier to eat the leftovers in moderation.

Avoid treats with sugar alcohols in them, specifically mannitol or sorbitol. They make the promise of being sugar free, but young children may experience bloating, diarrhea and a laxative effect, especially when eaten in larger quantities. And while sugar free may seem like a good idea for you, many are still loaded with calories and fat.

If you're still tempted, don't deny yourself. You can eat one piece, but fight the urge to binge with paper and pen. Make a resolution that before each piece of candy you eat, you have to hand write a 500 word essay on why you want it. Put down all the details of what you're thinking before taking a bite. Then project out how you'll feel after you've eaten it. But if your overeating opus grows to more than three volumes, you may want to skip temptation altogether and put the effort into finding a publisher.

As you finish writing you may realize you don't really want the candy after all. At the very least, it will take awhile to get that essay onto paper and you won't have enough time to eat everything in the bag.

Give everything away to the trick-or-treaters. Fill their bags up and you'll be fondly remembered as the cool house by all the neighborhood kids, and less likely to get toilet-papered during the rest of the year. If it's not sitting around the house it's a lot harder to indulge.

When that last kid comes to your door, give away everything that's left. Don't leave a couple of bars behind "just in case." When you're finished, turn out the porch light and call it a night. Candy out of your sight is likely to stay out of your mouth.

Should you have so much candy that you couldn't possibly give it all away, seal it up in a bag for work. Leave it in the kitchen area for people who take coffee breaks.

If you're the one who hangs out in the kitchen at work, see if there's a local shelter, halfway house, church or school that would like the candy. While you're at it put together some other things you've been meaning to donate like blankets, clothing, small appliances or furniture. Save your waist and trim down the clutter in your home at the same time.

If you're going to eat some, figure out how many calories you're about to take in. Are you just looking for a taste or do you want to pig out? A taste will give you something to savor, but eating an entire bowl of goodies will leave you with a sugar rush and guilt hangover. Set an upper calorie limit so you don't have regrets.

Now separate the treats into two piles, one that you like and another that you're going to give or throw away. When you're finished, put the reject candy in a bag and tape it shut. Then you should either throw it away or get it out of the house so you're not tempted. I like to put it in my car so I can drop it off at a local charity the next morning.

If you just can't bear the idea of throwing away food, and don't want to give it away, freeze it. Freezing candy helps it stay fresh for months and puts it somewhere out of sight. When you do take some out to eat, you're forced to eat more slowly because it's frozen.

Eat only the things you love. If you're a fan of caramel, don't fill up on calories from a lollipop. Eating nothing but your favorites will leave you more satisfied and less tempted by the treats that remain.

Arrange everything in the order you plan on eating it. Start with the best stuff, because if you put them last, you may eat through things you don't necessarily like to get to the "good stuff."

Put "roadblocks" in the middle of your candy lineup. Those are sweets that take longer to eat, forcing you to slow down. Suckers, hard candy and bubble gum can all act like roadblocks. Especially effective would be any of the small toys or gifts left over. Chewing through the plastic will certainly test your determination. (Just kidding about that last part!)

If you're really ambitious, do something healthy in between each treat. For example, after you eat a candy bar have a piece of fruit, jog in place for three minutes or do push-ups until you're too exhausted to put the candy in your mouth.

Don't start eating if you're working on the computer, watching TV or when you're on the run. Giving your attention to something else takes away from the enjoyment and makes it too easy to overindulge. Concentrate solely on the candy and eliminate outside distractions. Turn off the TV, the computer, unplug your phone, and make it worth your while.

Once you start eating, don't throw away the wrappers. In fact, you should line the empties up in front of you. Watching the pile grow can slow you down and act as a deterrent.

Once you've decided what you're going to eat, put it aside and get rid of the rest. If that means putting the excess in a bag and stomping on it or unwrapping everything and flushing them down the toilet, do it. Don't keep anything around to tempt you beyond what you've got planned.

Make a note of how much was left over so you don't buy so much next year, then stop feeling guilty about it. It looks much better in the trash than on your hips. Now you can enjoy your Halloween treat without it turning into a full-blown binge.

TAKE ACTION:
Don't buy candies or treats until the day
you need them. If they're not hanging
around, you can't be tempted.

Summary
Halloween

Before

Ask your neighbors how many trick-or-treaters you can expect. Only buy enough candy for what's expected.

During

Hand out everything you've got, don't hold back or keep any in reserve.

After

Get rid of the leftovers so they don't tempt you. If you're going to eat some, decide up front what and how much.

Flying
Coping Strategies

Airlines have always approached snack and meal time as a sort of necessary evil. In the past, they gave you the food, but on most airlines there wasn't much attention paid to the quality or the nutrition. They did it because they felt obligated, and the idea was to make it as inexpensive (for them) as possible, then hope that you ordered alcohol with it to offset their "loss." There were a few that tried to entice with higher-quality meals, but those were generally more expensive flights.

My how things have changed. The "necessary evil" food that they once gave away grudgingly, you are now expected to pay extra for. Most airlines will still give you pretzels, peanuts, or something else for free that will require an extra 15 minutes on the treadmill, but the days when airlines tried to set themselves apart with higher-quality fare are gone.

On the upside, this now gives you not only a health incentive, but a financial incentive to plan ahead. You can avoid all the fat, sugar and salt with just a little planning, and won't be stuck paying for the limited, and generally unhealthy choices the airlines give you.

Start your planning by contacting the airline, or visiting their website to see if your flight has any food or beverage service. Make sure to check the time of day you're flying. Some airlines don't offer meals at all, even on long flights, unless you're in the air during a specific mealtime window, or for a minimum amount of time.

If meal or snack service is offered, look for things like fresh fruit or salads with the dressings served separately. On breakfast flights frequently you can get a whole-grain cereal with low-fat milk. Avoid the bagel with cream cheese and skip the omelets, they're both loaded with empty calories.

A better option is to pack a meal ahead of time.

Make a peanut butter and sugar-free jelly sandwich on whole wheat bread.
Turkey or tuna fish tastes great when it's kept in a chilled carrying case.
Sliced vegetables, fresh fruit, raw unsalted nuts, low-fat granola and protein
bars all travel well. Hard-boiled eggs are good as long as you remove the
yolk. Low sodium and multi-grain pretzels or crackers can help you fight
cravings when they're passing out the snacks.

You can even pack an insulated plastic cup and spoon with some low
sugar instant oatmeal packets. When the flight attendants come around
offering hot water for tea, have them pour it over your oatmeal. Make it a
real treat by mixing in some chocolate protein powder and it tastes like a
dessert.

You will have to avoid bringing liquid protein shakes with you. Because of
the restrictions on fluids you'll be forced to leave them behind at security.
Also, don't chill anything with gel packs, since they aren't allowed through
either. Bags of ice are good alternatives because you can toss them out
before you go through the screening.

If you can't pack ahead of time, there may be some things you can pick
up at the airport before you start boarding. Fresh fruit is always a winner.
Beef jerky, even though it's higher in sodium, can provide some significant
protein. Sandwiches are available in many airports, but choose those without
cheese or mayo. Avoid sandwich wraps since many are loaded with
fattening sauces to keep them moist.

Remember to drink lots of water. Humidity is lower on a plane than most
homes, so it's easy to get dehydrated.

Finally, bring things with you to keep yourself occupied. One of the reasons
people eat while flying is out of boredom. If you're reading a book, playing
a game or watching a movie you're less likely to feel tempted by the
cookies they're selling.

TAKE ACTION:
Make a list of what you're going to eat at the airport, in case of delays and on the plane.

Summary
Flying

Plan Ahead

Make a special meal request when you book your ticket.

Bring your own food if healthy isn't an option.

Fight boredom eating with books, games and diversions.

Conclusion

So you may be wondering, "Is that it? I'm on my own?"

Far from it!

After working your way through this book you now know what your body needs, and why the one-size-fits-all diet plans aren't realistic. You've developed a set of workable goals, as well as calculated appropriate amounts of fat, fiber, protein and carbohydrates for a custom fit to your body and your lifestyle.

We've also shown you the most efficient way through a grocery store, and how to decipher the nutritional labels along the way. You've spent some time tracking what you eat so you know more about what you're putting in your body, and where there's room for improvement.

At the end of this book we've included tips on what to do when faced with situations where healthy options are fewer, and temptation is greater.

Don't stop now! Every couple of months, take this book off the shelf and re-read a chapter. Do the assignments again, keep the information fresh, and build on your successes.

But that's not all. We want to help you to move forward, so we've provided a number of FREE resources online.

www.DietisDead.com

Check this site out for help working through this book.

www.WeBeFit.com

This is our primary website packed with full-length articles on current health and fitness topics. Looking for more information on a particular subject? This is the place for you. We have dedicated sections on how to start a fitness program, new medical information, supplements, stretching and motivational articles. Subscribe to our free newsletter and once a week you'll receive an email with the latest information on our site.

www.WeCookFit.com

Instead of weighing the book down with meal plans, we've devoted another site to the hundreds of recipes we've been cooking, testing and posting online since 2004. They're broken down into convenient categories like breakfast, soups, salads, main dishes, desserts, protein bars and protein shakes.

The nutritional content of every one we post is checked to ensure it's a healthier choice. These recipes are higher in fiber, lower in sugar, higher in protein and lower in fat than traditional versions of the same recipes. Then each one is prepared and tasted by our panel to make sure it's something people would enjoy. If it doesn't taste good, we go back and try it again.

Some of these recipes have been through dozens of tries before getting approval from our panel (they're a finicky bunch). The picture you see is how it looked after a regular person cooked the final version. New items are posted every week, giving you a steady stream of healthy new recipes to try out.

www.FaceBook.com/WeBeFit

Once a week not enough? We also post daily tips on Facebook. Become a friend of WeBeFit and you can join in the conversation asking questions, making comments and interacting with other readers.

http://Twitter.com/WeBeFit

For those of you who want a daily tip that's short, sweet, and on-the-go, we also post on Twitter. Sign up for mobile updates and our tips will appear on your phone, wherever you are.

www.Youtube.com/user/WeBeFit

A few topics we cover can be a little complicated. To make possibly confusing ideas clearer, visit our YouTube channel for more in-depth demonstrations. A few of the topics we cover are antioxidants and free radicals, how to do a proper interval cardio session, correct form for the plank, and your resting metabolic rate.

So yes, this is the end of the book, but think of it as the beginning of your journey!

LaVergne, TN USA
15 December 2010
208934LV00001B/43/P